An Intimate Dialogue with God

Book 1:

The Miraculous Power of Unconditional Self-Love

Noemi Grace

ISBN-13:9781091806412

Set in Palatino and Helvetica
Designed and edited by Ellen J. Keiter,
Ellen's Arts, Wrentham, Massachusetts 02093

❊

For David

Without your tireless support and companionship,

this book would not be possible.

My heart overflows with gratitude and love for you

and your contributions to my life and work.

Love is the fabric of freedom.
Forgiveness paves the way to freedom.
You will know when you are free
when there is nothing left to forgive
because you see through the eyes of love.

—The Voice of the Oneness of God
March 3, 2012

Contents

Acknowledgments

My heart is full of love and gratitude for the Divine, who has chosen to bless me as a conduit for the words of love, wisdom and power in this book. Thank you for answering my prayer on September 11, 2001 with these priceless gifts. No words can express the depths of my appreciation for all you have done for me and for all you continue to do every day.

To my husband, David: you have been invaluable in transcribing, compiling, and editing the messages in this book. Without you, this book would not have been available for years. Your loving, wise contribution to this work is immeasurable. Thank you for really seeing me when we met so many years ago.

To the many communities in my life: I thank you for your acceptance and encouragement. To the Field of Dreams participants: thank you for embracing my quest to come out of hiding and share light and wisdom with the world. Little did I know at that time that my intention would manifest into so many gifts. To Sue: I thank you for your wisdom and generosity that made it possible for me to participate. To Dale: I thank you for your excellent facilitation, deep insight, and huge heart.

To the members of the Heartfield community: I have been blessed by your generous encouragement and receptivity to these messages. You have given me the courage to share these words with the world. I am in deep gratitude to you. Namaste.

To Dan, Jodi, and all the members of Your Soulful Book community: I am immensely grateful for your support, wisdom, and encouragement.

To Ellen: I thank you for embracing this message and me, and for your keen eye in editing and for designing this book and its cover.

To the beautiful souls who shared the Munay-Ki rites with me: you helped me open up beyond anything I could ever have imagined. I thank you.

To Janet: I thank you for our life-changing work together over many years and for seeing in me what I did not see.

To my parents, Ed and Eliana: I thank you for teaching me the importance of having a relationship with God. Your commitment to knowing the truth has shaped me into the person I am today.

To my sisters Ruth and Julie: I am grateful for your help throughout the years and love the beautiful women you have become.

I have learned from many teachers, and I am deeply grateful for all the gifts they brought to my life. I am indebted to Oprah and Deepak Chopra for their 21-day meditation challenges. They brought me to such a deep place that I could clearly hear God's voice speaking to me.

I am also in appreciation of the many women who have been in women's circles with me over the years and who have helped me grow and heal.

With a full heart, I send thanks to all of you.

Introduction

Have you ever considered that God wants you to love yourself unconditionally? I never did until God started to speak to me about how I could discover lasting happiness by loving myself in a new way, with Divine love as self-love.

I never expected to hear God speaking to me or thought I could love myself unconditionally. And I never could have anticipated that a heartfelt prayer uttered in the midst of a tragedy could have changed every aspect of my life. But it did.

The journey began the morning of September 11, 2001. I was stuck in a train station near Boston, shortly after terrorists hijacked planes originating in Boston, and crashed them into the World Trade Center in New York.

As I waited for the train for what seemed like hours, I saw fear on people's faces and felt it in my heart. At the station, which usually bustled with activity, the silence was deafening, my heart was racing, and I was trembling. I couldn't get the fiery images I had just seen on television out of my mind.

Never in my life had such terrifying events seemed so close; never was fear so palpable. As I stood immobilized by fear, it felt as if my heart was being ripped open. As I looked at my fellow commuters, my fright expanded to include them. I felt sheer terror for the people of the Boston area, where I lived, and for the people of New York City, where I grew up.

Fear engulfed me as never before, and the whole world seemed terrifying. I wanted to crawl into a hole and hide, but there was no place to hide. It was then that I uttered a pivotal prayer.

Because I grew up in a family that prayed daily, I had a fundamental understanding of prayer. But at the time, I felt spiritually adrift and I only prayed when desperate.

On 9/11, I was desperate and knew I had to pray, even if my prayer was never answered. In desperation, I spoke words I had never said before: "Use me for the healing of the world." I really meant those words and felt compelled to speak them for hours to keep the fear at bay.

For many years, I didn't speak of this experience and rarely considered it. But occasionally I wondered if my prayer would be answered, and why on that day I chose to meet fear with hope and willingness. As I have learned from the Divine,[1] that prayer is being answered through my becoming a channel for the messages in this book.

Over a decade flew by after I unexpectedly offered to be of service, and I thought about that prayer less and less. During that time, I began to work with a spiritual teacher.

As I worked on self-healing, I began to speak wise words to my psychotherapy clients that I knew were God's words and not mine. I never heard the words in my mind before I spoke them; they simply popped out of my mouth and surprised my clients and me.

Studying with the spiritual teacher gave me skills to help people heal their souls.[2] As a psychotherapist, I was trained to heal the mind and emotions. I never shared soul work with my therapy clients. I had compartmentalized

---

[1] In this book, I use the terms God, the Divine, and Spirit interchangeably. God is known by many names. These are the ones I generally use to refer to God.

[2] In this book, the Divine defines our soul as our timeless being.

my life so much that I was a therapist to most people and a soul healer to a select few who found me—despite my efforts to keep that work hidden.

In soul healing sessions, I was acutely aware of the need for Divine assistance and I began to listen intently for guidance. As I followed the directions I received in the moment, I was able to help clients heal deep issues that had not been resolved by psychotherapy.

This led me to pray for guidance when working with both soul healing and psychotherapy clients. Whenever I remembered to do so, I found myself speaking with clarity and wisdom that I knew I did not possess.

Over time, I also began to hear brief and powerful messages during my sessions with the spiritual teacher, which I could only attribute to Spirit because they were filled with love and wisdom.

Then on March 3, 2012, everything changed. That day began like most days. After breakfast, I turned on a recording of affirmations and hopped onto the elliptical. Partway through my workout, the affirmations recording suddenly stopped and I heard these words:

> "Love is the fabric of freedom. Forgiveness paves the way to freedom. You will know when you are free when there's nothing left to forgive because you see through the eyes of love."

Those marvelous words reverberated through the room and stopped me in my tracks. As someone who secretly harbored judgment and guilt, I knew those words were not mine. I also knew in my heart that they could only come from one source: God. Since then, the Voice that speaks to me has confirmed that it is the Voice of God.

Over the next few years, I occasionally pondered that message and tried to understand its meaning. Whenever I did, I felt deep peace. But the peace was short-lived and I was often consumed with the demands of daily life.

I began to focus on finding peace, and discovered that meditation helped me access inner peace. Then in January 2015, I began to receive messages from God during daily meditation. By hearing and recording these messages, I've learned many things, including the following:

- God loves us unconditionally and wants us to also love ourselves unconditionally.
- We each have a unique essence that is based in Divine love.
- God doesn't judge us and wants us to stop judging ourselves and others.
- God respects free will, but showers us with grace—especially when we invite Divine assistance.

Now the messages, which have had a profound impact on my life, are available in this book which contains transcripts of my dialogues with God. In this book, God speaks to all of us about the Divine's desire that we learn to love ourselves with God's love.

Each and every page of this book is infused with God's unconditional unchanging love. It is my hope for you that you will be touched and healed by these loving words.

For me, learning to love myself in the Divine way has been truly unexpected and freeing. Yet I know that I am a work in progress and that I am no more special than any other person. I have also learned that we are all uniquely special to God.

My own unique experience is that I uttered a prayer that had profound consequences. I also honed my ability to listen through years of working co-creatively with the

Divine to help clients and in sessions with a spiritual teacher.

We all can learn to listen to God because God is speaking to all of us. The messages in this book are an opportunity for us to deepen our listening. As you read the beautiful words that God shared with me, you will learn how you can liberate yourself through loving yourself with Divine unconditional love.

Before I introduce you to the Voice of the Oneness of God which has changed me to the core, I'd like to share a few words about the organization of this book to help you have the best experience while reading it.

This is the first book in a series of books that contain transcripts of my communication with God. Each book in the series bears the title *An Intimate Dialogue with God* and contains a unique subtitle. This first book, subtitled *The Miraculous Power of Unconditional Self-Love,* presents the Divine's perspective on the experience and power of Divine love as self-love.

The remaining books in this series contain messages from the Divine on:

- God's perspective on forgiveness (which is very different from what I thought) and how forgiveness paves the way to freedom;
- living in presence as the foundation for lasting happiness and solution to life's challenges;
- how to invite and receive the blessings of Divine grace and assistance in a new way; and
- the purpose of our lives within the context of the soul's journey to love, wholeness, and oneness with God.

The messages are organized into chapters by topic, rather than chronologically. I've also added a title to each message, highlighted points for reflection, and suggested practices at the end of each chapter.

For clarity, the words in the remainder of this book are presented as follows: the Divine's words are indented; my words, thoughts, and reflections are not indented.

Now it's your turn to hear God speaking to you about how you can live a life filled with Divine love and grace through experiencing Divine love as self-love. I invite you to turn the page and listen with an open heart and mind.

An Intimate Dialogue with God

Book 1

Book 1: The Miraculous Power of Unconditional Self-Love

In this first message, God highlights the key points addressed in this book, and speaks to me in the plural, using the word "we." This is intentional, and the Divine explains why in the first chapter.

The following words were spoken to me by the Divine:

> The journey to freedom starts with loving yourself with Divine love. When you love yourself with our love, your love never wavers. The only love that truly frees you is Divine love, which is unchanging and unconditional. We don't love you more when you exceed your expectations, and we don't withhold love from you when you make choices that lead to painful outcomes. To us, you are always lovable.
>
> In this book, we teach you to love yourself as we do—unconditionally and consciously—which is contrary to how the ego loves. When you love with ego's limited love, your love varies according to the conditions of your life, the stories you tell yourself, and how you feel and perceive things. That type of love never frees you, but Divine love does. We have a new love story for you: loving yourself fully with our unconditional conscious love. Become

conscious through loving yourself with Divine love. Our love experienced as self-love frees you in ways you can't imagine.

First, you must learn to see differently and choose differently. We will teach you to see from love and choose from love. This way, you apply unconditional love to your life, which transforms you and your life. In the process, you become more like us, as you learn to love yourself unwaveringly and unconditionally.

This transformational process liberates you from your past, your stories, and the limitations you have believed about yourself. It also unearths the truth of who you are and helps you become whole within yourself. As you return to wholeness, your connection to us grows. All of this is possible and is the journey your soul—your timeless being—has longed to complete.

Allow us to be your guide to self-love and freedom. Will you choose us, as we have already chosen you? We delight in helping you to discover the true purpose of your life as you learn to live in self-love and express your unique essence through self-loving choices. Are you willing and ready to learn? We love you and always receive you with open arms. Namaste.

1

The Voice and the Choice

Quotes from the Divine

God is here, available and ready to work wonders
in the life of anyone who is willing.

Be open to experiencing what lies outside
the boundaries of what you think is possible.
[This] creates the potential for opening
a storehouse of energy, a vortex of creativity,
and opportunities you could not
have seen beforehand.

Messages from the Divine

The Voice and the Choice

After receiving loving and uplifting messages for months, I finally got the courage to ask to whom I was speaking. With trepidation I inquired, "Who is speaking to me?" The answer blew me away:

I am the Voice of the Oneness you call God.

Is the Voice of God separate from God?

The Voice of the Oneness of God is not separate from God. But we have many attributes: love, wisdom, kindness, gentleness, boldness, compassion, caring, and many more. We also use many forms of communication, including: visions, voice, knowing, seeing and hearing. You are being blessed through your hearing, knowing, and believing in that knowing.

I feel blessed, and I am grateful that I hear you. Why do you use the word, "we" to refer to yourself?

God is one and many at the same time. We are fullness, yet always expanding.

I know the words you speak to me are true, but why me? What have I done to deserve this blessing?

You are being blessed because of your desire, not because of your doing. We heard your authentic and willing prayer on 9/11 that you uttered without ego: "Use me for the healing of the world." We are using you because of the cry of your heart to be of service to those in pain. We always delight in receiving those who desire to be of service.

We also watched with glee when you watched the *Conversations with God* movie and your heart echoed the desire, "I want to have conversations with God." Again, your heart spoke without ego. Now we speak to you and through you.

We have heard you and watched your commitment to working on yourself and to learning to have a healthy relationship with ego. We are always looking for vessels that desire to serve without ego, willing to be divinely gifted without claiming those gifts as their own brilliance. Yet you are all brilliant when you live your true essence, but few live as the beauty of their unique essence.

Noemi, we honor your commitment to communing with us each day, and we are delighted with the growing time and heart you bring to our connection. You are a willing recipient and we are also blessed in sharing this time with you.

You are blessed in communing with me?

Noemi Grace, your light is bright. You will use it to help guide others to their own light, brilliance, and wisdom. Simply be the beautifully brilliant soul that you are and listen. Be willing to hear truth even if it seems to contradict what you learned in the past or what your mind thinks is true.

Practice giving your mind a vacation every day in meditation and prayer—not in endless petitions—but in thanksgiving and fellowship with us, the Divine Source of life.

Noemi, you are a voice, a listener and repeater of truth. Your soul has wandered from truth, as all have. Now you are being called to trust on a greater level, to open to new possibilities and new ways of being, to live in gratitude and service as a light in the world. We honor your prayer to be of service for the healing of the world.

How do I know when I am hearing the voice of God?

Jesus said that you shall know the truth and the truth shall set you free. If what you hear sets you free, it is truth. The one Divine Source is universal Truth. This Truth can be experienced in so many facets that it may appear to be many, disparate truths. Yet God is both one and many at the same time.

How do you want me to share these words?

You leave that to us. Your job is to receive and keep yourself as a clear channel for these words. We ask that you share these words with those around you who are open; they will be blessed by your sharing.

For now, rest in the comfort of receiving, and know that your comfort zone is rapidly expanding. All is being prepared and will be opened for you. We will show you the doors and open them. You only need to walk through the open doors.

The world needs to hear that God is here, available, and ready to work wonders in the life of anyone who is willing to be of service. There is no need to struggle to make it happen. Trust us and allow us to be gentlemanly with you, opening doors and walking through them with you, arm in arm. We are the miracle workers, so you need not be. You have requested miracles, so hang on. We are brewing a new batch of miracles for you that will manifest soon.

We are here for you, working 24/7, as you would say. You are here to be an example of all the grace and riches available to all who ask with a pure and open heart.

We love the open heart, innocence, and trust you bring to your time with us. Thank you for this. We are refreshed every day in our communication together. Many have been waiting for the message of love and choice we are gifting you. We are delighted you have chosen us.

I have chosen you? I thought you chose me, and I didn't understand why you would choose me.

You chose us first with your prayer. Now we are graced together with you in this communication. An open heart is a gift beyond words. Live in your heart. Make this a goal every day. There is no need to strive for this; simply choose it.

We love you as a dear friend. Thank you for your willingness to be of service. Everything you desire will be yours, starting with peace and joy.

This dialogue left me with tears flowing down my face. What a gift to hear such profoundly loving words! Through my ongoing communication with the Divine, I am learning that God wants to bless all of us, and that the greatest blessing we can ever receive is more of God's Love and Presence in our lives.

"We Are" Is the Same as "I Am"

I have learned that you are the Great I Am. Is "We Are" the same as "I Am?" I assume this is true, but I don't want to assume anything.

Yes, we are the Great I Am, the only I Am, the fullness of I Am. As the fullness of all that is, we are. We use the plural in speaking with you to emphasize both our oneness and fullness. God is oneness and fullness—that is who we are.

In speaking with you, we are reminding you of both who you are and who we are. God is one and many at the same time. We are not many gods, but one of many, one that is many, like your body, which is also one of many—of many cells, many organs, and many parts.

We are one composed of many—one that is the fullness of many. This is who we are. This is also who you are part of when you return to the fullness and wholeness of who you are, in connection with us.

We are one and many; that is not a contradiction. We function with the wholeness, fullness, and oneness of the one and the many, as does your body, but on a much fuller scale.

We love you, Noemi Grace. We love every one of you humans that we have created in love, through love, and as love. And in your wholeness and fullness, you too are love.

We are the God you have always known —not just you, Noemi Grace, but all who read this. Yet we are much more than you have ever known or imagined us to be.

Your world is replete with God-in-the-box religions. Yet we are too big to be boxed. Are you willing to see outside the box, to become unboxed as we are, to see both us and yourselves in fullness?

We delight in sharing our fullness with you. And we invite you to drop the boxes in which you have placed both yourselves and us. Are you ready and open to discover much more about yourselves and us than you have ever known? This is the invitation, gift, and blessing we offer you today.

Bring the Horizon Closer

The following message came to me early in my ongoing communication with the Divine. The words surprised me, yet they turned out to be quite prophetic:

Be open and willing to experience what lies outside the boundaries of what you think is possible. You recently closed a long chapter in your life. The closing of every chapter creates the potential for opening a storehouse of energy, a vortex of creativity, and opportunities you could not have seen beforehand.

Open wide to the opportunities before you. Recognize the beauty and wholeness in everything, even when things break apart. Love and support are all around you. Do not get caught up in what is not love, beauty, grace, or support. Recognize it and choose to bring your gaze to the love and grace all around you.

You have opened a vortex of newness beyond where you have been, and the possibility to quantum leap there is before you. We now speak to you and you hear us. It is through the greatest breakdowns that the biggest breakouts are possible.

Focus on what lies just beyond what you think is possible. With focused energy, you bring the horizon closer, and what you thought was impossible becomes possible. Then you manifest with ease, grace, beauty, and wholeness.

Love is the fabric of freedom and the antidote to fear. Love is present, here and now, ready and willing to fill you to overflowing. Will you receive it? Embrace love, even for what you don't like or understand, and do not forget to love yourself.

Do not judge anything about your situation. Loss creates an opening, a vortex for new growth that was not possible beforehand. The relationship you recently left needed adjusting. How you perceived that relationship kept you from seeing, appreciating, tapping into, and receiving the love all around you from other sources.

This has been a difficult lesson for you. You did your best to focus on being love, while speaking your truth. We commend you; we know it was hard. Open wide to the beauty, grace, and newness around you and within you. Beauty and grace are who you are. We love you, and we share our peace with you.

This was one of the first messages I received from the Divine about self-love. At the time, I was in emotional and mental pain, and I could not begin to fathom the depth and meaning of these words.

This message refers to my decision to separate from a spiritual teacher with whom I had worked for years. She was not only my teacher, she was my best friend. I truly believed that I needed her to hear God speaking to me, as I had begun to receive messages from the Divine through our work together.

I agonized over the decision to walk away. But staying in the relationship had become increasingly painful. I knew in my heart what I needed to do. Yet I was terrified, and I expected to be lost, lonely, and devastated by making this decision.

But by the time I spoke up, I somehow understood that this was not about me being right and her being wrong. From where she stood, she was correct; from where I stood, I was doing what I needed to do out of self-love. For the first time in my life, I was able to be grateful for the gifts that I received from a relationship, while choosing to walk away in self-love.

I have learned from the Divine that my choosing from self-love and my ability to perceive her, myself, and the situation without judgment were major factors in being ready to be a channel for these Divine messages.

After making that painful decision, wonderful changes that I did not anticipate began to happen in my relationships, both with friends and with my husband. And I didn't expect that after a lengthy separation, my connection with my former teacher would be renewed and that both of us can now see and appreciate each other from love.

Now my heart yearns for you to also be blessed through receiving God's love, choosing from self-love, and hearing God speak to you.

The Big Picture

This next download presents the big picture of the Divine's perspective on this book and provides a framework for understanding ourselves and our lives. I invite you to open to perceiving yourself and your life with this understanding.

> You are being gifted a series of books, beginning with a trilogy on love, wisdom, and power.[3] We have spoken on these before, but our emphasis in speaking with you is different. The meaning we ascribe to these words is beyond your understanding, and the context in which we share them differs from your ordinary perception.
>
> You perceive yourselves as individuals, with your own struggles and goals. While this is true in your reality, you are so much

[3] For the first publication, the Divine messages on love are being published as a series of books. This book on the miraculous power of unconditional self-love is the first in the series on love.

more. You are part of us, yet in your experience, you are separated from the truth of who you are, and you perceive that you are separated from us. In separation, you feel isolated and alone, and you do not realize that you are part of a greater whole.

In your wholeness and fullness, which you have not yet experienced, you are uniquely love. The closer you get to the truth of who you are, the less isolated you will feel even when physically alone.

These books are an invitation and guide for you to return to wholeness within yourself and to oneness with us. The invitation is for all of you to join us on a journey to the truth of who you are and to your true essence which is unique and birthed in love.

The journey begins with learning to love yourself in the Divine way: unconditionally and consciously. In this experience of Divine love as self-love, you return to wholeness and the truth of who you are. As you do, your unique essence and beauty shine from you, your connection with us grows, and you increasingly receive Divine grace. Through returning to self-love, self-truth, and self-knowing, you also acquire wisdom and power.

The only reality you have known for so long is separation. All that you desire, but feel unable to achieve or receive, has been caused, at least in part, by your lack of unconditional self-love and by your separation from yourself and from us.

Many of you desire oneness with us, yet you rarely experience it because you are separated within yourselves. You must first become whole within yourself; then you can grow into oneness with us.

We are here to support and guide you on this journey to full self-love, wholeness, and oneness with us, your Divine Source. This is the journey you have been waiting for all your life that your soul longs to complete.

Will you choose this journey or be open to it? We invite you to join a mass migration of humanity moving away from non-love and separation to love, wholeness, and oneness with us. We will be your guide if you are willing, and we desire to do so.

Your Journey to Self-Love and Wholeness

This download explains the purpose of this book series within the context of the larger framework provided by the previous message. It also explains the process of Divine love as self-love and the purpose of our lives from the Divine perspective. Every time I read these words, I am deeply moved.

This book series is about Divine love and grace filling your hearts and minds, and saturating you until you become love and grace. It is about returning to your Source, which is Divine love, and to your unique pure essence, which is also love.

By this process, you become yourself in wholeness. Until now, your wholeness has been hidden under layers of ego wounds and protection. Love gently peels away the layers to reveal the light, beauty, brilliance, and power that you are. As Divine love and grace flow through you, you become a beacon of hope, a fountain of wisdom, a well of compassion, and a rainbow of acceptance.

The first thing you must realize is that you are not who you think you are. Your true essence is the essence of God, and this essence is within you.

The heart of who you are is Divine unconditional conscious love, sown as a seed into you and expressed as your unique essence. You can choose to nurture the seed with self-love and self-acceptance, or you can neglect it and let it shrivel up through self-rejection. You nurture the Divine seed through loving yourself in a different way than you have before—not with ego's love, which is filled with conditions and laced with judgment—but through Divine love which is pure, unconditional and conscious.

Receiving our love and allowing it to spread in you and flow out of you nourishes you and nurtures others. This is what it means to say, "My cup runs over."

Allow Divine love to flow from you, without withholding it or restricting its flow, and you become love. Then you also invite Divine love as grace into your life to transform you, fill you to overflowing, bless you, and bless the world through you.

When you live this way, every moment is sacred and everything is precious. You delight in life and share your riches with others. Life becomes a miracle and you are the miracle you always had the potential to be. Problems dissolve or are easily solved. Your perspective opens to new possibilities, and you no longer focus on the things that led to anxiety or depression. You are no longer needy for love from others because you are filled with our love and share it everywhere, and that fills you even more.

Even those around you can also be transformed by the Divine love flowing out of you. You become complete in love, live in wholeness, and participate in wholesome relationships with whole people.

Through this process, you become blessed and happy. The life you once knew seems a distant past. You live in the present as your pure essence of love and grace. Your future opens in ways that amaze you. You become a fountain of love and a channel of grace, transforming hardship and suffering into love and grace. But first, you must live in a different way that invites Divine love and grace into your life.

Let us help you to transform your life into one in which suffering ends and happiness expands. We are helping raise the vibration of humanity through these words. We are grateful to those who choose to return to their Source, true nature, and unique expression of love. The opportunity is available to all of you, and this book can guide you home. We are always here to assist you. Will you ask for our help?

Applications:

These Divine messages have helped me in many ways. Every day I'm learning more about how to: stop judging and rejecting myself and others; deepen self-love; and sweeten my relationship with God. As you read the rest of this book, you will have the opportunity to apply these messages to your life, so you can experience Divine love as self-love firsthand.

Points for Reflection:

- The heart of who you are is Divine unconditional conscious love sown into you and expressed as your unique essence.
- If you allow them, Divine love and grace will fill your heart and mind until you become love and grace.
- Through the process of returning to your Source and pure essence, you become yourself in wholeness.
- The journey to wholeness begins with learning to love yourself the Divine way: unconditionally and consciously.

- You are being invited to join a mass migration of humanity from non-love and separation to love, wholeness, and oneness with the Divine.
- God's love as Divine grace is always available to help transform your life from suffering to happiness. You only need to invite it.

Practices:

- Create pockets of love in your day through self-care and self-loving choices.
- Check in with yourself throughout the day. When you discover you are not being self-loving, stop and soak up God's love in meditation, prayer, or simply breathing in love.
- Become more aware of when you are suffering, and choose to invite Divine help.

2

The Love Filter

Quotes from the Divine

The greatest tragedy is
that you do not love yourselves unconditionally
and you see most things and live every day
through your primary filter of self-judgment
and victim consciousness.

Through self-love, a whole new world awaits.
Self-love is the portal
to everything you desire and more.

My Experience: From Anxiety to Peace

On January 1, 2015, I boldly wrote the following statement in my journal: "My intention for this year is to embrace what is and reclaim my joy." Little did I know that three days later I would start to receive messages from God that were filled with Divine love, wisdom, and grace.

At the time, I was fed up with being in an anxious frenzy each week about money. I wanted to be at peace with my financial situation, but no matter how hard I tried, peace was fleeting and joy was even more elusive.

Over the years since 9/11, I made my relationship with God a priority and I viewed myself as a spiritual person. Yet the truth is that I didn't trust God to take care of me. This led to angst on a weekly basis and guilt over my inability to trust.

Although I was often riddled with anxiety, I was also blessed by experiencing daily peace in meditation, which I began with my husband in October 2014. I also experienced peace when asking for Divine assistance in working with my psychotherapy clients. Although I experienced daily pockets of deep peace, I didn't trust outside of those times, and I was often in inner turmoil.

I knew the solution was to embrace what is. But I kept trying and failing. I also wanted to learn to be happy. At the time, I didn't think of myself as unhappy. I had healed a lot of sadness and loss over the years, but that didn't lead me to lasting happiness, and moments of joy were fleeting. I decided that I would reclaim my joy, although I didn't know how to do so.

Three days after I boldly stated my intention for the year, my unexpected journey to self-love started with two simple questions from God, to which I still return today. Every time I answer them, my perspective shifts from judgment to love for myself and others, and embracing what is becomes much easier.

An Invitation

I invite you to use the messages in this chapter, including these two questions, to help you see your daily struggles, your life, yourself, and others with eyes of love.

Messages from the Divine

Powerful Questions

"I want to embrace what is and reclaim my joy." I wrote that statement in my journal and was surprised when I clearly heard this response:

Practice embracing what is. This is where miracles happen; life becomes a miracle and anything is possible.

Make your life a miracle by asking and answering these questions throughout the day. Doing this helps you to see your life from love. Over time, this will completely change your life. We refer to these as your **operative questions**:

1. **What do I see when I look at this from love?**
2. **What do I choose if I choose from love?**

When you perceive anything in life as challenging, ask yourself these questions. They will bring you back to love and you will see life with eyes of love. When you do, everything in your life will change.

Are you willing to do this and allow us to help you find freedom through love? Beauty, joy, and love await you. Namaste.

Choosing from Love

How can I make more self-loving choices?

See yourself as a conduit of love. The highest vibration is unconditional love. Do you believe that love heals?

Love conquers all?

Love does not conquer, fight, or resist anything; love melts, heals, and enlivens.

Fill yourself with Divine love. Don't block or reduce the flow of love. See your struggles through eyes of love and your challenges as opportunities for more love. Make this your ultimate goal for now: to love what is.

Remember this always: Love is the fabric of freedom; forgiveness paves the way to freedom. Learn to forgive yourself of everything you think you've done wrong and let it all go. When you see through eyes of love, you see there is nothing to forgive.

Open wide and feel deep compassion for yourself. There is nothing wrong, bad, or inferior about you, and nothing is broken or needs fixing. You will see your own perfection when you stop to look at yourself through eyes of love.

Every moment is an opportunity to choose love. Every pain, whether physical or emotional, is a reminder to choose love. Keep choosing love, then one day you will realize that love is choosing you. Actually, love chose you long ago to be the beautiful soul that you are. Let love flow into you, through you, and out of you. This choice makes all the difference on your path.

Choose from love; this will simplify your life. What do you choose when you see your life, relationships, health, and finances from love?

Everything appears different when seen from love. When you choose from the perspective of love, your experience also changes: you enjoy life more; connect more with people who love you; and you care more, love more, and live more.

Develop this habit: when you have a decision to make, ask yourself, "What does love choose here?" It's all choice. What do you choose when you choose from love?

You are love and your loving presence transforms your world. Fill yourself with love until you overflow. Then let go and let love. This means to let go and let God, for God is love.

Choose love; this is where miracles happen. Allow love to transform the landscape of your life from barren to fertile, struggle to bliss, and lack to overflowing. This is all possible with love.

Love What Is and Magic Happens

I notice I judge myself and others less when I use the operative questions. I also have a lot more compassion. One thing I have no compassion for is the chronic foot pain I'm experiencing. Some days every step is painful. How can seeing and choosing from love help me with this?

Your feet hurt because you don't feel supported by the Universe, when nothing could be further from the truth. There are four things you need to remember and keep in your awareness, if you wish to heal your feet:

1. We love you. Learn to see everything with eyes of love, as we do.
2. We always support and buoy you. Never forget this.
3. Lack is an illusion; abundance is real. Jesus came so you would have abundant life. Where in your life don't you perceive the abundance that's already here?
4. Joy is your purpose for being. You are here to reclaim your joy. All else will flow powerfully from joy. Learn to live in joy. Bring joy to all of you, including your body, and don't forget your feet. Life without foot pain is possible for you if you learn to live in love and walk in joy.

Are you saying that if I live this way, my foot won't hurt—that love, joy and changing my perspective can heal my foot?

Yes, that's exactly what we're saying. But it won't happen overnight because your foot pain is here as a daily reminder to help you learn to see and choose from love, and to live in joy.

Learn to ascend above all problems. You see things as problems because you do not see from love. Everything you perceive as a problem is an opportunity to see from love. When you see from love, everything looks different because your view has changed.

Self-love is the road to the life you desire. As you walk the road of love, you find you only desire what is. You forget other desires and love what is. But before you get to that point, you must make different choices. Yet once you love what is, magic happens and your life becomes a miracle. You even become a miracle; then everything is possible.

Learn to love what is and embrace it like a loved one. Hold it, then release it, and open to enjoy the next moment, and the next. By living this way, you can become a blessing to yourself and others.

As I began to practice seeing and choosing from love and experiencing more joy, my foot pain lessened—and now it rarely hurts. I have been able to hike and enjoy walking, and I don't take my feet for granted anymore. When my foot does hurt, it always reminds me to refocus on love and joy, and to take time to appreciate the Divine support and abundance all around me.

Change Your Filter, Change Your Life

I'm starting to experience the power of the love filter. Can you tell me more about filters?

You live your life through your filters. You filter what you see into perception, and virtually every experience in your life has been filtered. Even love is filtered through your idea of how love should be. The only unfiltered experiences are unconditional love and oneness, which for most of you are rare experiences.

Profound transformation occurs simply by changing your filters. Have you ever considered that you can filter your life through unconditional love? Have you ever stepped back from a situation to look at it from love, instead of from your thoughts and emotional reactions? When you see from love, everything changes. It is also easier to heal and transform your life with love than with any other method.

You will be amazed when you take your eyes off people and events, and see what your filters have prevented you from seeing. All judgment stops when you see from self-love and embrace self-acceptance. When you do not judge yourself, you have no need to judge others.

Self-love is self-freeing; it offers freedom to you and to others. Liberate yourself with self-love. When we speak of self-love, we always mean Divine unconditional love experienced as self-love.

When you see through the filter of this love, your perception changes: you see beauty; you experience compassion where you had judgment; you see possibilities where things looked hopeless; and anger and judgment disappear, leaving you with peace and joy.

Change your filter, and you change how you perceive and experience everything. You do not have to work on changing your thoughts because they flow from your filter.

I like this. I've tried to be aware enough to change my thoughts. But I often don't recognize that my thoughts are non-loving until I've been stuck in judgment for a while. This sounds like a much easier way to change my thinking. I can use the love filter instead of trying to figure out if my thoughts are healthy.

Yes, that is true. Change your filter and your perception changes with it. Instead of filtering what you see through the lens of non-love, you can learn to filter through the perspective of love.

When you change your filter to love, you also make different choices because you are motivated by love. Become aware of your filters, and consciously choose to see from love.

We delight in teaching you to see from unconditional conscious love, as we do. We are here to help you to become fully conscious and change your vibration from judgment to love.

Judgment is rampant in your world and is fully entrenched in your minds. We can help you free yourself to return to love and to the truth of who you are. Then you will discover you are much more than you ever thought you were.

This journey begins by changing your perception and seeing with eyes of love. Use your operative questions daily. Then you can learn to love yourself as we do: unconditionally and consciously.

With this one change, you can transform your entire life. When you see from love, every choice is different, and when you choose from unconditional love, your experience is radically different. Through self-love, a whole new world awaits. Self-love is the portal to everything you desire and more. Will you walk the road to self-love with us?

Change Your Filter, Change Your Story

When you change your filter, you change both your life and your story. Your story is how you describe your life inside your mind and to the outside world.

Most of you live a story that you don't like. You see most things through your primary filter and live as if your filtered perspective is absolute truth. It is absolutely not truth, though for you it is real because you only see what you filter into your perception.

You live a story that can be a comedy or a romance, but is mostly a tragedy. The greatest tragedy is that you do not love yourselves unconditionally, and you see most things and live every day through your primary filters of self-judgment and victim consciousness.

Through the filter of self-judgment, you reject yourselves. Through the perspective of victim consciousness, you blame others, justify, rationalize, and tell a story about everything.

You continue to live the same story even when other characters in the story change. As you experience new relationships, jobs, and events, the same patterns of hurts, betrayals, and abandonments emerge, and the new story is a repeat of the old one.

Learn to filter through love instead of through judgment and victimhood. When you apply the love filter to your perception and actions, you begin to see and choose from love.

Over time, your filter will change from judgment-based to love-based, and your story will change from victimization, "poor me" and rejection to "I love myself enough." What a wondrous day it will be for you when you live a love story in which you love yourself unconditionally and live from self-love.

When you change your filter to love, you change your life. You stop wandering down the road that leads to self-judgment, self-rejection, and victim awareness. You also become aware of many wonderful things about yourself and your life that you previously didn't realize.

This happens because you changed your filter, and in doing so, you changed your story. In your new story, you live in love, wisdom, and power, and not in judgment and victim consciousness.

We always support the transition from judgment and blame to acceptance and love. We are here to help you live sweet lives of love and acceptance. You only need to invite our help.

We live in love, as unconditional love. And we invite you to take the journey to learn to love as we do.

Say Goodbye to the Victim

Your mind is often occupied with thoughts, worries, and judgments that don't serve you, and even cripple you. You must learn to leave behind all the demeaning, diminishing, and punishing things you say to yourself in the privacy of the mind. You must see how detrimental this is and learn to recognize that inner judgmental and doubting voice when it speaks to you.

That voice is not your true voice; your true voice is a voice of love, like that of an angel. Yet you rarely hear it because your mind drones on with rotting garbage. Have you tired of its stench yet? Are you weary of the criticism and self-loathing?

Are you willing to learn to embrace the love that you are? It is possible to transform yourself from self-loathing to self-loving. And it is your birthright to love yourself and live as the love that you already are deep down inside.

Divine love experienced as self-love heals. If you desire this above all else and spend a little time with us daily, or even a few times a week, everything in your life would shift. You would move out of the slow lane of non-transformation into the fast lane of full transformation and freedom.

If you want to live in freedom, you must stop indulging yourselves in your minds and stop being victims. Most of you delight to be victims. This is difficult for us to understand.

Many of you embrace your perceived powerlessness with such vehemence. You find strength in being powerless and you perpetuate that powerlessness by seeing yourselves as victims. You are very attached to your victimhood. You say you hate it, but you also find a false sense of strength and vindication in it.

Freedom is here now, but not for the victim. Victims can never love themselves unconditionally. They are too attached to their wounds to see the true beauty and love that they are. Give up the victim; tell it goodbye.

Choose love or choose victim—it is that simple. For most of you this is difficult, because you are attached to being victims and you perceive most things through the lens of victim awareness. Drop the victim filter and choose the love filter. Instead of seeing through the eyes of the victim, choose to see from love.

Remember, your operative questions: What do I see if I look at this from love? What do I choose when I choose from love? You must love yourself enough to choose from love.

The victim is not motivated by self-love. Its perspective is always clouded by its wounds and it cannot see past them. You are beautiful, unique, and special. You come from the Divine Source, yet you live in the squalor of victim consciousness.

Victim awareness runs very deep. You have no idea how much you perceive things through this mindset and how limited you make yourselves because of this. You think your circumstances and the people in your life are what make you limited. But you do this to yourself by choosing to be a victim.

Victims can never know the truth of who they are. They are blinded by their perception of powerlessness. One of the greatest tragedies of human existence is that you believe you are powerless, when you are actually very powerful.

The true source of your power comes from Divine unconditional love. Since you do not love yourselves unconditionally, you do not experience the fullness of this energy source. You are like a depleted battery with only a little power. That is the unfortunate reality of the victim's existence.

You can recharge your batteries easily and effortlessly by leaving behind the victim and returning to self-love and to the truth of who you are. If you feel powerless, you have lost sight of this truth. Being a victim is as far away as you can get from the truth of who you are.

You have let the powerless victim run your life instead of living from your unlimited power source, which is love. Make the decision today to return to love. When you choose from love instead of victim awareness, you can live in the richness of the beauty and brilliance that you are. And you will live as the truth of who you are: powerful and beautiful love.

Commit to living the truth of who you are by saying goodbye to your constant companion, the victim. Don't hate the victim; love it and let it go by choosing from love. The victim is incompatible with unconditional love. Choose love, not victim. It has had its time. Now is the time to become the truth of who you are. Make this your mantra and reality every day: Love, not victim.

We see the beauty and love that you all are, and we delight in the opening and unfolding of who you are. We are always here with you in love.

Applications:

Over time, the operative questions have transformed most of my close relationships. These questions have been like a magnifying glass that highlights the love in others and allows me to see their vulnerabilities, as well as my own, with compassion instead of judgment.

Through the operative questions, I shifted from debilitating fear about my financial situation to embracing my circumstances and developing a deepening trust in the Divine's ability and desire to take care of me. This has been truly liberating for me. Even though my circumstances have not changed, I'm learning to trust the Divine. What a relief!

The operative questions help me to realize when I am resisting or trying to control aspects of my life. Then it's much easier to let go and laugh at myself.

What aspects of your life would benefit from applying the love filter?

Points for Reflection:

- Love does not conquer, fight or resist anything; love melts, heals, and enlivens.
- Practice embracing what is. This is where miracles happen and your life becomes a miracle. When life is a miracle, anything is possible.
- There is nothing wrong, bad, or inferior about you, and nothing is broken or needs fixing. You will see your own perfection when you look at yourself from love.
- Every moment is an opportunity to choose love, and every pain is a reminder to choose love.

- When you see things as problems, it's because you aren't seeing from love.
- Everything changes when you learn to see from love, as God does.
- You are supported and buoyed by God all the time. Never forget this.
- Lack is an illusion; abundance is real.
- Joy is your purpose for being. You are here to reclaim your joy. Learn to live in joy.
- All judgment stops when you see from self-love and self-acceptance. When you do not judge yourself, you have no need to judge others.
- When you change your filter to love, your story is about love, wisdom, and power instead of self-judgment, self-rejection, and victim awareness.
- When you change your filter, your perception and experience of everything changes. You don't have to work on changing your thoughts because they flow out of your filter.
- When you change your filter, you change your story. When you change your story, you change the way you live your life.
- You can change your perception to love by using the operative questions daily. Then you can learn to love yourself unconditionally and consciously, as God does. With this one change, you can transform your entire life.
- Victims can never love themselves unconditionally or know the truth of who they are.
- It is your birthright to love yourself and to live as the love that you already are.

- One of the greatest tragedies of human existence is that you believe you are powerless, when you are actually very powerful.
- The true source of your power comes from Divine unconditional love.

Practices:

- Make your life a miracle by asking and answering these operative questions throughout the day:
    1. What do I see when I look at this from love?
    2. What do I choose if I choose from love?
- Make this your ultimate goal for now: to love what is.
- Develop this habit: when you have a decision to make, ask yourself, "What does love choose here?"
- Make this your mantra every day: Love, not victim.

3

Love Yourself First

Quotes from the Divine

If you do not love yourself,
you miss the entire point of life.
Love is why you are here.
Love is the truth that sets you free,
but only when your love includes you.

Most of you miss the one direct path to happiness:
falling deeply in love with yourself,
not with the ego's conditional love,
but with Divine unconditional conscious love.
You cannot be in love with yourself and be unhappy.

My Experience: Learning to See Differently

As I started to shift my perspective to love by using the operative questions, I began to see things differently. I also realized that my lack of self-love was a serious detriment to my life. The choices I made often emphasized others' priorities or needs over my own. Over time, I became more focused on doing for others than on honoring and caring for myself. As I began practicing seeing and choosing from love, I also started to care for myself in a whole new way.

Then one day I was shocked when I heard the Divine telling me to love myself first. This is contrary to what I had learned and I even argued with God about this. But since then, I have learned that the Divine wants us to love ourselves in the same way that God does: unconditionally and consciously. And when we do, we can love ourselves and others without judgment. This continues to be a daily journey for me, as I learn to choose more from love and become increasingly uncomfortable with judgment.

Through our dialogues, God gave me a simple statement, called a context, which has helped me make the self-loving and self-caring choices that I feared or avoided in the past. Using the context even empowered me to make a pivotal, yet painful choice that deeply opened me and led to the unfolding of this book. At the time, I had no idea where my choice would lead me.

An Invitation

I invite you to apply the context statement, along with the other teachings and practices in this chapter, to facilitate making self-loving choices and to experience Divine love as self-love for yourself.

Messages from the Divine

Love Yourself in a New Way

Love is the fabric of freedom; love is the substance of which freedom is made. You cannot be free if you do not love, or if your love does not include you. If you wish to be free of the judgment, pain, and sorrows that you carry with you, you must love yourself. There is no freedom without love.

How do you define freedom?

The most basic experience of freedom is to fully love, know, embrace, and be your true self. When you live in non-love, you carry shackles of judgment and pain with you, and you are powerless to free yourself from them. When you love yourself with our Divine unconditional love, our love empowers you to free yourself.

How can we get to freedom from where we are? How can we learn to love ourselves if we don't?

You all must learn to see and love differently. Most of you love yourselves in a conditional way at best, and many of you don't love yourselves at all.

The problem is not that you are unlovable, but that you believe this is true, so it might as well be. In your belief that you are inherently unlovable, you become unlovable to yourself. We love you unconditionally, and you are not unlovable.

The problem is not you; the problem is how you love yourself. Most of you have not learned unconditional self-love because your experience of unconditional love has been limited.

The love that brings you into freedom is not the ego's version of love: I love you until you disappoint me, or I love you when I think you are worthy of love. Freedom is sourced in Divine love, which is both unconditional and conscious. We, as your Divine Source, always love you.

When you experience the opening to freedom afforded to you by Divine love, your fears fall away. What many of you fear most of all is what is inside you. We will show you the truth of who you are, if you allow us. And this will amaze you. You all have love and beauty inside you that has been bottled up and buried. The truth is that every one of you is beauty at your core.

What you think you see inside yourself is a distortion. What you believe to be true about yourself and your life blocks you from seeing the truth. To see the truth of who you are, you must learn to see from love instead of from judgment, past assumptions, and conclusions.

When you see from love, everything changes. This doesn't mean you see love where it's not present. But it means that you see the love you have been blind to until now. You see yourself in a new light, and you easily fall in love with yourself. From here, your entire life changes: you bloom, your life blossoms, and you become happy.

This is our promise to you: if you fall deeply and unconditionally in love with yourself, and see the truth of who you are and live that truth, you will find a deep happiness you cannot imagine now. This is possible for every one of you.

We invite you to journey to freedom. Let us be your guide to unconditional love and the truth of who you are. Then you can easily make self-loving choices, further deepening your love for yourself. Through those choices, you become whole and create a life you love.

Will you join us on this magnificent journey to self-love and wholeness? We never tire of being your partners on this journey. We love all of you and we delight in showing you how to love yourselves, starting with teaching you to see yourselves from love. Are you game? We await your answer in love and grace.

Get Out of Your Way with Self-Love

You are all in your own way because you don't love yourselves unconditionally. To get out of your way, you must learn to love yourself unconditionally. The best way to do this is to tap into Divine love and love yourself with it. Divine love is the only love that is the fabric of freedom.

When you love yourself this way, it melts the resistance you have to fully being you. Most of you have a lot of resistance. But when the resistance melts, you allow your powerful light to shine as a beacon for those in the darkness of non-love. Love is light; everything that is not sourced in love is born in the darkness of fear.

Love yourself first with Divine love.

You want me to love myself first?

Yes, but you can't do this from ego. Until you move beyond ego, even for a minute, you can't love yourself this way because ego doesn't know this kind of love. Learn to love yourself first without ego.

How can I love myself first without ego?

Saturate yourself with Divine love and reflect it first inward to yourself and then outward to the world. This eliminates all self-loathing and violence towards self and others. Are you willing to do this?

I'm willing to try.

There is no trying. Simply connect with us every day in meditation and prayer and receive our Divine love and Divine gifts. We are here with you always. You must learn to receive first and then do. We love you and honor you.

Rise Above the Human Condition

Can you tell me more about how we can we get out of our way?

You get out of your way by being willing to see and do differently. You each repeatedly make the same choices as you continue to see with the same distortions.

Be willing to ask: "What am I not seeing here?" and "How am I contributing to this?" When you ask different questions, you will get different results. Many of you do not ask yourself questions. You go through life with blinders on, reacting to what happens, and trying to control anything and anyone you think you can control.

The mind drones on endlessly with the same distortions every day because it sees with blinders on. Only the heart can see without blinders. Learn to ask yourself thought-provoking questions, and answer them from your heart. Ask deeper questions of yourself without attaching judgment or blame to anyone. Stop avoiding, rejecting, and judging yourself, and seek to know yourself more fully.

Be willing to ask and you will receive answers that you can't imagine. You, Noemi, started by asking questions about yourself and being willing to: see yourself in a different light; discover deeper truths about yourself; and go to what you called "a scary place." Then you discovered beauty and grace pouring out of you into your life.

I remember the feeling of going to that "scary place" of truly looking at myself. I was sure I would see that all the things I judged about myself were really true. I saw myself as harsh, judgmental, and unlikeable. But when I saw past my judgment of myself, what I saw was surprisingly beautiful.

The journey to self-love starts by asking yourself better questions. Stop asking, "What is wrong with me?" and "Why is this happening to me?" Start asking, "What do I see when I look at this from love?" and "What do I choose if I choose from love?"

Be willing to know yourself. You cannot love what you do not know, and many of you fear knowing yourself because you think you are ugly. Yet if you dare to get to know yourself, you will discover your unique, astounding beauty beneath the judgment, blame, harshness, and rejection you carry.

You are all beauty at your core, in your essence. Yet you think you are ugly and feel shameful and guilty. This is the true tragedy of the human condition. We will teach you how to rise above the human condition, to go deeper than the judgmental layers you have stacked upon your true essence. When you dive deep into yourself, you will be astonished to find someone beautiful, amazing, and gifted.

But to get there, you must ask yourself deeper questions. Be willing to look at your part in things and take ownership. Don't be afraid of looking at your limitations. You must stop rejecting the limitations you carry and learn to embrace them before you can see how truly unlimited and magnificent you are.

You are afraid to look at imperfections. But it is in doing so that you discover the truth of who you are. Deep down beneath those surface imperfections lies the most amazing beauty you can imagine. Yet your fear of those imperfections keeps you from discovering your true perfection: the beauty, grace, and love that you are. And we speak to all of you here.

Fear nothing; love is stronger than fear. If you are in fear, return to love. In love, you see that everything you have wanted from others and from life lies within you in seed form. Nurture those seeds in love. Learn to see the love that you are. Then you will live in beauty, joy, and peace. And non-love will have no power over you.

The Journey to Self-Love

Love is the starting point of the journey and fullness of love is the endpoint, yet there is no end. The moment you realize that you do not love yourself and you choose to learn to love yourself is a key moment that takes you down a new path. On this new path, the strategies you used in the past to control your life no longer work and being a passive bystander in your life leaves you stuck.

Here happiness is within your reach if you learn to choose from love. Some of you have given up on happiness, and others try to take happiness into their own hands by attempting to control everything.

Most of you miss the one direct path to happiness: falling deeply in love with yourself—not with ego's conditional love, but with Divine unconditional conscious love. You cannot be in love with yourself and be unhappy.

Many of you chase feelings of happiness you experience in new relationships. When you fall in love with someone you accept everything about them, even things you know will be a problem for you in the future. You are filled with feelings of love and everything seems perfect. Imagine feeling this for yourself. You cannot imagine this experience of perfection that you can have in falling in love with yourself because you fell out of love with yourself long ago.

We are here to remind you that the path to lasting happiness is the path to self-love. If you want sustained happiness—not just brief happiness in new relationships, jobs, children, and vacations—you must love yourself. Yet you have sought happiness in every other form except self-love. You even shudder at the possibility of having to love yourself to experience lasting happiness.

All is well in self-love; happiness resides here. Are you willing to take this path?

Yes, I am. What is the next step?

Ah, the next step. You always want to know what's next. Is self-love not enough?

I know it's enough, but somehow I always think there is more for me to do.

All you need to do is love yourself. There is sweetness in this place of self-love.

Along the journey to unconditional self-love, you acquire wisdom and power. You come to realize that everything you thought you knew was distorted by a lack of self-love, and you recognize that true power is sourced in love.

You are here to experience yourself in your unique wholeness, beauty, and fullness. You are also here to leave separation and rejoin us in oneness in our true shared home in unconditional love. This is not an overnight journey. You have been separated from yourself and us for a long time.

The journey to self-love is about returning home to you. As you start to gain momentum on this journey, everything changes. You embrace in pure acceptance things you judged and life begins to flow easily. In this process your perception changes. You see the sun shining and the sky is no longer gray even when it rains. This is not the ungrounded bliss of falling in love. This happiness is sweet, sustainable, pure, and sourced in your experience of Divine love as self-love.

We salute all who have chosen this journey. We are here to assist you in every way and welcome you with open arms. So much magnificence awaits you. We invite you to journey with us to our home in love and oneness.

Love Yourself First

Self-love is the foundation for the full expression of the beauty and grace that you are. You have forgotten to love yourself into wholeness and to care for yourself as the most important person in your life. To forget to love yourself is a serious crime against yourself. Stop hurting yourself with non-love.

Let go of self-judgment and learn to see both the judgment and what you judge through eyes of love. Then you can have compassion for the place in you that is too wounded to love. Love all of you with boundless self-love. Every day receive Divine love into your heart, and allow it to grow and flow into all of you and out to others.

Noemi, you are capable of loving many people, but you must also love yourself. You are a gracious, loving presence. Grace is who you are. Noemi Grace means sweet grace. Be that to yourself first. You are a gift; be the gift to yourself first.

It's hard for me to own this.

It's only hard because you judge yourself. Stop judging and choose love as the foundation for your life. Don't try to correct or change anything that is not love. Simply see from love and learn to resist nothing, judge nothing, and attach to nothing.

Then you can see with true perspective and live in the miracle of love, where everything is possible. Love is part of the solution to all your challenges. Everything you desire manifests easily when it flows from love.

Love yourself first, as if you are all that is. Make this is your mantra: Remember self-love. Self-love is self-freeing when you love yourself fully and freely. Let all you do flow from love. Love yourself and let everything else go.

Wow, this seems contrary to what I've learned. It seems too selfish to love myself first.

Loving yourself first is not selfish or hard when you see and choose from love. Remember to use your **operative questions**:

"What does this look like when I see it from love?" and **"What do I choose if I choose from love?"**

Remember, self-love is most important. Every day complete this phrase, **"I love myself enough to . . ."** We refer to this phrase as your **context**. What do you love yourself enough to be or do? Answer this question daily, then be it, and do it.

If you do not love yourself, you miss the entire point of life. Love is why you're here. Love is the truth that sets you free, but only when your love includes you. Love yourself where you are and in whatever you do. Let your love grow, first for yourself, and then for the rest of the world, and you will transform your whole life.

The context, "I love myself enough to . . ." has been life-changing for me. I've made some radically different choices through using it.

In particular, it made my decision to stop working with the spiritual teacher, who was also my best friend, very clear. Before I had this tool, I anguished over the decision. I feared being judged and losing my friend, and I felt stuck. The context helped me to look at the situation very differently, and then it became crystal clear what the most self-loving choice was for me. It also made it much easier for me to let go of the fear I felt about making the decision. And I was able to release the judgment I was holding. I never could have anticipated how that decision paved the way for me to receive the Divine communication that I'm sharing in this book.

Honor Yourself in Your Choices

We have another practice for you. Daily, ask yourself, "What would I do differently if I loved myself unconditionally?" Then go ahead and do it.

I don't think I know what it means to love myself unconditionally.

To love unconditionally is to accept everything in love without judgment, blame, story, or games. To love yourself unconditionally is to know yourself in the depths of your being, and embrace yourself with full acceptance without judgment. Pure love and full acceptance can transform anyone and anything.

When you experience unconditional love and acceptance, you easily know the difference between being love or being in story and ego. In love, you don't need to fix, change, or explain anything, and you reject nothing. Unconditional love and acceptance can free you to make different choices than you did in the past.

Love yourself enough to honor yourself by your choices. When you love yourself unconditionally, you don't abandon or betray yourself through non-loving choices, and you are unwilling to choose what dishonors you or others.

You may choose to walk away from someone or a situation, but you do so without judgment. You leave, because to stay would not be self-loving. Yet you have no need to blame others or to defend yourself. You simply see from love that you must leave. Once you know this, the choice is simple.

Will you love yourself enough to free yourself by choosing differently? To love yourself unconditionally is also to honor yourself by choosing what takes you into deeper self-love and acceptance. It is to step into your power and exercise that power in making choices that honor you.

Honor yourself daily for the remarkable being you are. This takes you deeper down the path towards loving yourself with Divine unconditional love, as we do. This is to live in beauty.

We honor you for your choice to be with us. Now honor yourself in how you live your life.

Choose Differently from Self-Love

How can I be more at peace, serene in my circumstances, not caught up in frustration, or sweat the small stuff?

Serenity radiates from a loving heart. Love yourself, love those around you, and also love your circumstances.

I have a harder time loving circumstances than people.

You want to control circumstances and you can't. Serenity comes from surrender. We see more of that in you, as you wonder with great amazement at where we are taking you. You are coming along with us, without any idea or attempt to control. We love that in you.

Live this way in your life. The road of life takes you through twists and turns you can't imagine: ups and downs, peaks and valleys, and fertile and drought times. You cannot control any of this.

The need to control comes from ego, which cannot accept what it cannot control. Ego resists things that it cannot manipulate or it does not understand. See the ego's attempts at control, and choose from love instead of ego.

Look at your life circumstances from love. Ask yourself these questions, "If I loved this, what would I do? If I loved this, how would I be different? What do I need to let go of so I can love this?"

Always remember to use your operative questions, "What do I see if I look at this from love? What do I choose when I choose from love?" And remember your context, "I love myself enough to. . . ."

Love yourself enough to let go. The ego fears letting go because it thinks its survival will be threatened. Yet it is always safe, if it doesn't interfere with you loving yourself unconditionally with our love.

Human unconditional love, not sourced in Divine love, is short-lived—"I love you unconditionally until you disappoint me." Divine love is eternal and always freely flowing.

Love is the answer you have been seeking. We are not speaking of the needy, clingy thing you humans call love, or the demanding, expecting version either. Our love, which never varies or falters, is always present. Source yourself in Divine love and let go of control. Love and let go—in that order. See everything with the eyes of love, then let go.

In love, you desire the best for you and others, and you trust that you will receive what is best for you, even if it isn't what you wanted. You receive what life offers, and also what others do, without judgment. This doesn't mean you sit by and allow yourself to be abused. Remember your context.

If you love yourself unconditionally, you choose differently than if you love yourself partially: you find a way to honor yourself; you do not choose against yourself; and you see more options because you reject nothing and embrace everything.

We notice your resistance here. You're thinking that no one should embrace abuse. We said embrace, not condone. From a place of acceptance and love, you choose what is best for you. Sometimes resisting abuse keeps people stuck in receiving abuse because they don't accept what is. They may not identify what is happening as abuse, and make up a story that paints a different picture.

Your stories keep you mired in the past and distracted from the present, so you cannot see what is truly here. Who would you be without your story? Begin to tell the story of your life from love. Start with self-love, and expand your story to include love of others and of life.

Remember that the self-love we always speak of is sourced in Divine love, flowing inward to you, and eventually outward from you to the world. What the world needs is this kind of love that it rarely sees. We are grateful for those who choose to love this way.

Love Yourself Consciously

Love is our essence and yours. We are conscious love—fully aware and present, and fully love. We love you unconditionally and consciously. When you awaken to your true essence, you too can learn to love yourself consciously.

Human love is often unconscious and conditional; we love both consciously and unconditionally. You must be conscious to love yourself consciously. To be conscious, you must be aware, know yourself, and be at home within yourself. Most of you can't be at home within yourself because you fear what lies within.

Conscious love is liberating; it places no conditions or demands on anyone. It is present, full, and free-flowing. When you love yourself first with our love, you can love others unconditionally, and your love for them will never be non-self-loving.

Love between two conscious people fills them both. When you love unconsciously, you can use your love to attempt to buy another's love, and your love is laced with expectations or neediness. Conscious love recognizes how much unconditional love a person can receive and gives in a manner that they can receive. It doesn't smother or make demands for love, yet it gives without expectation and is never depleted.

Some of you may think that you love others unconditionally. But your version of unconditional love is unconscious if you lavish love on selfish people who do not return your love or who give you crumbs. You love so much because you desperately want to be loved. When your love is not reciprocated, you become hurt and try harder to win the other's love. This is not conscious.

In a conscious relationship, two people love each other in a way that frees both without neediness or selfishness. Conscious love is impossible with selfishness or self-lessness. The selfish person mostly takes;

the selfless person mostly gives. Thus neither experiences the mutual flow of love between them. You may think that being selfless is the highest form of love. At times it is, such as the love of a parent for a young child. But selflessness as a way of life is damaging. How can you return to your true self if you discard yourself in selflessness?

Reclaim yourself and become who you truly are. Seek to become self-full—fully your true self living your true essence, which is love. Stop abandoning yourself in selflessness; stop stealing love in selfishness. As long as you are selfish or selfless, you will never experience lasting happiness.

The path to happiness is found in loving yourself unconditionally and consciously, accepting yourself, and discovering the beauty of your pure essence and sharing it with the world. Love yourself first with our unconditional conscious love and you can't help but find happiness.

You Love Others How You Love Yourself

You love others in the same way that you love yourself. If you love yourself unconditionally and consciously, you will love others unconditionally and consciously. To love this way is Divine.

If you love yourself conditionally, you actually judge yourself in your loving. Then you only love yourself when you perceive yourself to be successful, beautiful, perfect, or okay enough. As long as you meet the standards you or others have established for measuring yourself, you feel lovable and you love yourself.

If you love yourself in this conditional way, you have no basis for unconditionally loving God or anyone else. You will resent yourself, others, and even us for the failures you perceive through your default filter of victim consciousness.

See consciously with eyes of unconditional love, and your perception changes completely. Hear with ears of unconditional love, and you hear yourself and others differently.

Unconditional love is truly priceless and rare. To become unconditional love is the greatest aspiration. When you love God, yourself, and others in this way, you will experience peace and many blessings.

See the Beauty Within

Today I'm judging myself for reacting in anger to something my husband said. I don't like feeling this way. Please help me.

When you see from love, you perceive that everything is either love or a desperate cry for love. When you see this way, you have no need to judge anyone because you understand that non-loving behavior results from being desperate for love. When you see this way, you can see others and observe their inner beauty, and even their vulnerabilities and defenses, from love.

Love yourself first with our love. To do so, choose to receive our unconditionally flowing love whether you are content or you feel badly. Recognize the cry for love hidden in the discontent and love yourself even more. When you learn to love yourself this way, it's easy to turn those unconditionally loving eyes on everyone else.

You are easier to love than you think you are because you *are* love. When you see from love, you see who you are, and you see the purity of your heart. Jesus said, "Blessed are the pure in heart, for they shall see God." When you get to know the purity, beauty, and compassion of your heart, it is easy to see others in the same light.

For some, their beauty is buried deep. Help them find the truth of themselves. You are divine and so are they, but they might not know it yet. Help them to know themselves as love. This is the path to freedom.

There are many paths to freedom, but the path through love and grace is a shortcut. We honor your choosing this path and sharing it. We have already seen this come to fruition and appreciate your commitment with love. We both are love together as we share this beautiful dance of life.

Applications:

As I shared earlier, using the context, "I love myself enough . . ." has helped me tremendously. In addition to enabling me to make a pivotal choice to close the chapter with the spiritual teacher, it continues to help me to make smaller loving choices every day. When I forget the context and operative questions for a while, I notice that I become increasingly judgmental and inflexible, my life becomes imbalanced in the direction of work, and self-care and fun go out the window. For me, self-love leads to balance.

Recognizing both my own desperate cry for love when I'm irritable, and my husband's when it seems he's being critical of me, has dramatically decreased the small arguments we frequently had. Our friends used to call us the Bickersons. Recently, one of them declared how much more enjoyable it was to be with us since we became the Graces instead of the Bickersons.

When seeing with eyes of love, we can both recognize the desperate cry in each other. Then we can offer compassion and connection instead of judgment. This has restored the emotional intimacy that was lacking for years in our relationship. We have been blessed by receiving and applying these Divine messages.

Where in your life could you benefit from choosing what is most self-loving? Where have you been missing the desperate cry for love within yourself or someone else? How could your life be different if you responded more from love?

Points for Reflection:

- The tragedy of the human condition is that many people think they are ugly and feel shameful and guilty, when the truth is that the essence of each of us is beauty.

- When you don't love yourself, you are in your own way.
- Forgetting to love yourself is a serious crime against yourself. If you do not love yourself, you miss the entire point of life. Love is the truth that sets you free, but only when your love includes you.
- Love yourself first with Divine love. You can't do this from ego. You can only do this by being saturated with Divine love, reflecting it first to yourself and then to others.
- To love yourself unconditionally is to know yourself in the depths of your being, and to embrace yourself with full acceptance without judgment.
- To love yourself unconditionally is to honor yourself by choosing what takes you into deeper self-love and acceptance.
- Love yourself enough to let go of control. See everything with eyes of love, then let go.
- If you love yourself unconditionally, you honor yourself by the choices you make.
- Human love is often unconscious and conditional. Divine love is always conscious and unconditional. To love yourself consciously, you must first become conscious.
- In a conscious relationship, two people love each other in a way that frees both without neediness or selfishness.
- Selflessness as a way of life is damaging. Seek to be self-full—fully your true self living your true essence.
- Most people miss the one direct path to happiness: falling deeply in love with themselves. The path to lasting happiness is the path to self-love.

- The path to happiness is found in loving yourself unconditionally and consciously, accepting yourself, and discovering the beauty of your pure essence and sharing it with the world.
- The journey to self-love is returning home to *you*.
- When you see from love, you perceive that everything is either love or a desperate cry for love.
- If you love yourself conditionally, you have no basis for unconditionally loving God or anyone else.
- Choose love as the foundation for your life. Love is part of the solution to all your challenges and everything you desire manifests easily when it flows from love.

Practices:

- Take time daily, in meditation and prayer, to be saturated with Divine love, and then reflect that love first to yourself and then outward to the world.
- Make this your mantra: *Remember self-love.*
- Every day complete this phrase, "I love myself enough to. . . ." And be willing to do whatever the answer is.
- Ask better questions and you get better results. Be willing to ask, "What am I not seeing here?" and "How am I contributing to this?" Stop asking, "What is wrong with me?" and "Why is this happening to me?"
- Every day ask yourself, "What would I do differently if I loved myself unconditionally?" Then do it.
- Look at your life circumstances from love. Ask yourself, "If I loved this, what would I do? If I loved this, how would I be different? What do I need to let go of to love this?"

4

You Are Uniquely Love

Quotes from the Divine

Learn to see yourself from love
and choose what is self-loving.
Then you will start to see the true beauty of your essence
and you will fall in love with yourself.
You can't imagine this, yet this is available to you
through Divine love experienced as self-love.

Your true self is unique.
Will you deprive humanity of your flavor of Divine love
that will never be known again?
Or are you willing to live from
the depths of your being?
One person living this way can change their world.

My Experience: Discovering My Essence

Applying the love filter impacts me on a daily basis. Sometimes I'm unaware of its power until I realize that I'm approaching a situation, another person, or myself differently than I did in the past.

In the deepening dialogues with the Divine, I've learned that each of us has a pure essence that is sourced in love. At our core, we each are a unique expression of attributes of Divine love, and we are not our egos.

I have been shocked to discover how far off my perception of myself was from the truth of who I am. I have always perceived myself as harsh. But as I grow in self-love, I'm discovering and appreciating the beauty of my pure essence, and I'm becoming the truth of who I am, as a gracious loving presence.

It took me quite a while to be able to claim that and know that it is true. Now, remembering this truth helps me to move from judgment to love, and has significantly diminished the anxiety that used to have a stranglehold on me.

An Invitation

I invite you to open to discovering your unique essence through the Divine words in this chapter. You may be amazed to discover who you truly are. Loving yourself as your unique essence can also help you free yourself from anything that diminishes you.

Messages from the Divine

Your True Essence Is a Flavor of Love

I awoke one day with new sense of who I am and wrote the following words in my journal:

> I see with the eyes of the heart. I see love.
> I hear with the ears of the heart. I hear love.
> I speak with the voice of the heart. I speak love.
> I choose with the heart. I choose love.
> I am love. Love is who I am. Love is my essence.

The Divine response to these words offered great clarity and compassion:

> Yes, your essence is love. Your true self is a sweet flavor of love. Consider love as ice cream and each person as having a unique flavor of love. Each is unique, but it's all ice cream, and it's always sweet. Love is who you are. There is no point in denying it.
>
> Noemi, you are a gracious, loving, wise essence; this is your flavor of love. Each person has their own flavor of love, and they can discover it through loving themselves. Seek to share your flavor of love and to enjoy the sweetness of others' flavors. Love flows into your heart from us, your Divine Source, and out of you through your flavor of love.
>
> Ego is a distraction and detraction from unconditional love. The ego does not live in unconditional love; it lives in separation and attachment. Ego craves specialness, but is also scared for its survival. Separateness tries to keep you special: your ice cream is not just ice cream; it is ice cream plus sprinkles, toppings, and sauce. To the ego, separateness is necessary for surviving people and things it doesn't trust. The ego does a dance between separation (It says, "I am different from you.") and attachment (It says, "I need you to love me, to take care of me, to tell me I'm special.")
>
> Unlike ego, the true self only needs love and connection. It recognizes its oneness

with God and others. It does not need to stand out in the crowd; it already knows it's special. What a wonderful place: knowing, feeling, breathing, and living your own specialness.

How special you all are! If you would see this, ego would not need to exist. The ego is a construct of the mind that masks your true Source, which is God, and it projects its idea of its specialness into the world.

Your true self is an extension and expression of Source. As you grow into your essence, you become fully grounded and expanded at the same time, like an ever-growing tree. Yet you have wings to fly and soar above the mundane. You perceive that love is all around you and in you. You express love through your choices and share love with everyone through your connection with the Divine Source of love.

When you see through eyes of love, everything else fades away or is transformed. Your life becomes beautiful and filled with love. Remember to see it this way. Unconditional love makes life worth living and is the reason for living. You are here to expand into love and to express that expanded love in your uniqueness. Open wide to receive our love and equally wide to share it.

Give away the riches of your flavor of love whenever you can. They are God's gift to the world through you when you share them. You will be blessed many times over. You are loved, dear one. See the love, hear the love, taste the love, and speak the love. You are a voice to speak this message of love, wisdom, and power. "I am love." is a great mantra for you. Live love and love life; it is that simple.

Live love and you can't help but enjoy life and attract more love, beauty, grace, and abundance. This path to abundance is what you have been seeking. Love is the fabric of freedom. Love is here now. Let love lead the way. See with eyes of love and follow love. In what direction is more love? Go in that direction. Live in love, but more importantly, live as love.

You are blessed and a blessing to the earth. We thank you for your willingness. Blessings to you, now and always.

Your True Self Is Sourced in Love

I love what you shared in the last message. But I'm a little confused. Is the true self the same as the true essence?

The true self is the part of you that is sourced in the one truth of unconditional love—in the truth that God is love and at your core, you, too, are love. Your true essence is your particular flavor of Divine love. Your true self is love, yet its essence is a unique expression of love. Some in their essence are love, whereas others may be joy, peace, or other Divine attributes that flow from love.

Your true essence expresses a unique blend of attributes of love. You can discover your essence when you connect with us in meditation, prayer, or a deep healing. There is a depth to you, yet you only know the tip of the iceberg, and only scratch the surface of the beauty, love, and brilliance that you are. Many live their whole lives without knowing who they are.

To discover who you are, begin to recognize the aspects of God that you experience when you deeply connect to us and to yourself. Your true self is unique. Will you deprive humanity of your flavor of Divine love that will never be known again? Or are you willing to live from the depths of your being? One person living this way can change their world.

Live with us in the essence of your being—in the essence of your uniqueness with our Divinity. Live this way and you will know beauty, joy, peace, abundance, or whatever you desire. Of course, what you desire changes as a result of living from your Source in Divine unconditional love. We love you and ask you to hold this awareness in your life.

You Are Not Who You Think You Are

Many of you feel separated and isolated, and a sense of loneliness permeates your being. You do not realize that the root cause of your aloneness is separation from your true self and your Divine Source. Most of you live in separation, disconnected from your pure essence, which is deep inside yet seems unreachable. You are unaware of your unique expression of Divine love. And you have lost your connection to your true self, which is within you, but might as well be in another galaxy.

You are not who you think you are. Many of you reject your greatest gifts and see yourself as the opposite of who you are. Many deny their brilliance, compassion, loveliness, kindness, and uniqueness, and try to blend into the background. And some try to assert their uniqueness, thinking themselves better than others.

Both perspectives are inaccurate; you are no better or worse than anyone. Your true selves are all born of the same Source, which is Divine unconditional conscious love. You have all become disconnected from that Source. As a result, you are also separated from yourselves. Who you are is magnificent. Yet you will never know this unless you restore your connection to your true self and Divine Source.

Your journey to wholeness starts with learning to love yourself as we do. Spend time with us, receiving our love and filling yourself with it. Then meditate on "I am love." Allow these words to penetrate the layers the ego has constructed around your heart and they will start to melt in love. Receive our love and remember: "I am love." Declare it, own it, and allow yourself to be it.

When you are frustrated, sad, angry, or disappointed, practice claiming, "I am love." This helps you to return to love. Over time, as you own "I am love," that message becomes "I am peace," "I am compassion," "I am joy," or whatever your unique flavor of Divine love is. Through this practice, your unique essence grows brighter.

You all have been sourced in love. Start owning this truth by declaring, "I am love." Claim your essence as love and allow your understanding of who you are to unfold. Knowing who you are banishes all self-doubt and allows you to live from your essence. Then everything changes without struggling, striving, strategizing, forcing, or planning. You simply move into the vibration of who you are.

Here is the big picture: in your pure essence, you are love; and you are returning to your true essence and true home, which are love and oneness with us, your Divine Source. We delight in your returning home. Regularly spend time with us and everything will fall into place as if by magic, as you effortlessly become who you truly are.

Love is the starting point and endpoint of the journey. It is both the solution and the way to the solution. Love is here now. Are you? Will you embrace our love and love yourself with our love in a Divine embrace of love and kindness? Be kind to yourselves. That will make the journey easier. We love you always, for all time and beyond.

Remember Who You Are

I'm happy to be in your presence again. Can you help me understand the difference between the ego and the true self?

You have all become confused about who you are, and you mistake yourselves for your egos. In identity confusion, you see everything from the ego's perspective and filters of victim consciousness, entitlement, and self-preservation. You live in a box of the ego's creation and your perception is bounded by the walls of that box.

If you live in your ego, you cannot live in the power of your pure essence. In your confused identity, you live a life limited by past experiences. Everything that happens occurs within the boundaries set by the past and the ego's assumptions and conclusions.

Ego is always concerned about survival, but it does not recognize that the best way to ensure your survival is to see and live from love. When you see yourself as your ego, you limit yourself tremendously and the only possibilities you see are based on your past. Despite your best efforts to do things differently, you drag your past into the future because you only see with the perception and filters of the past.

Ego also likes to make choices that give it a sense of control. When you live from love instead of ego, you don't waste your time trying to control things you have no power to control. Whenever you feel the need to control, you are in ego, deepening your self-amnesia.

You have all developed amnesia about who you are, and the cure for this is to return to love, to see from love, and to choose from love. The ego primarily chooses from preservation and entitlement, not love. An easy way to know if you are in love or in ego is to look at the motivation for your choices. Are they loving of yourself and others or are they self-centered and controlling?

The deeper you are steeped in ego, the greater your amnesia. The cure for this amnesia and the path to restoring your memory of who you are is through love. Practice seeing and choosing from love, and it becomes easier for you to recognize when you are not in love.

When you see from love, you have an undistorted view. This doesn't mean that everything you see is pretty. When you see from love, you see the truth of something or someone. By knowing that truth, you are empowered to make self-loving choices.

When you apply the love filter to your life, your vantage point opens up beyond the confines of the ego's boxed perception. Learn to live from love, and your life will grow in ways you can't imagine, as you are liberated from your past. Everything you want awaits you when you live from love, though what you want may change when you don't see from the ego's boxed view.

To see outside the box, you must see from love and especially see yourself from love. You end your identify confusion by remembering who you are, experiencing Divine love as self-love, and embracing your unique essence.

Start to see ego as not you, as not your true self. Learn to identify who is talking and choosing, and who you are being in the moment. When you see from love, you know the difference between being in ego and living the truth of who you are. When you restore your perception of who you are, you will be liberated in many ways.

You are magnificent beings of love and beauty. To see this, you must stop seeing from the ego's boxed view and start seeing from love. For now, continue to use the love filter, return to your operative questions and context, and choose from love.

Then one day, you will recognize yourself for the first time, and you will know yourself as love, compassion, joy, peace, kindness, or other attributes that are based in love. As always, we love you and are here to help you.

Discern Your True Self from Ego

Ego limits you. Ego is not bad and it has a necessary place, but that place isn't as the dictator of your life. To allow ego to control your life is to choose to live a life of limited possibility, repeating the choices of the past.

The new and expanded life you desire is possible when ego serves as your true self's helper. The ego's true place is to be in service to the true self: to come to action upon the command of your true self, and to be otherwise at rest. An ego at rest: that may sound like an oxymoron, and in a sense it is because few rise above its dictates and needy behavior.

The ego craves acknowledgment and it looks to others to provide it. It does not realize that no one can give you what you already have but don't see. If you truly knew your magnificence, you would never need anyone to give you validation. Beneath the layers of ego and beyond the wounds that pockmark your soul, lies the infinitely bright light of your true essence that nothing can snuff out. But ego doesn't see it.

The ego is also fearful of looking at limitations and imperfections because it fears its own demise. Your true self is unafraid. The ego does not realize how much beauty is beneath its perceived imperfections, and it's too afraid to look. If you are avoiding or rejecting any aspect of yourself, you are in ego. The ego rejects everything it fears; love fears nothing and embraces all.

Learn to recognize when you are in ego. Then return to your true love essence and everything will change. It is only in owning all the limitations and imperfections that the ego fears that you can reach the beauty and magnificence beneath them. When you own your perceived imperfections and limitations, they no longer own you or have power over you. Then you are able to see them for what they are. You recognize that they are not your true self, which is perfect in its beauty. Everything else is simply layered on top of your true pure essence, and is not who you truly are.

Discern the true self from the ego. This is very important. Be willing to be of God and not of ego, to walk on the earth and be of the earth, but not tied down to it. Learn to be non-attached, yet fully open and loving. It is a remarkable journey you are embarking on. We honor and love you.

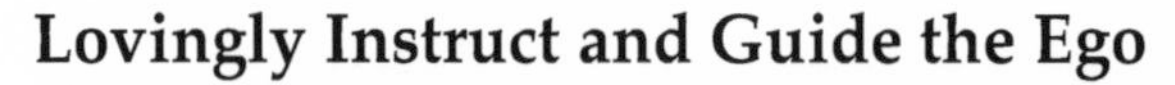

Lovingly Instruct and Guide the Ego

Is it possible to transcend the ego in this lifetime? What is the highest and healthiest relationship with ego?

> Love the ego; do not exclude it from love. See it through eyes of love. Ego's top priority is your survival. What do you see when you look at your ego from love?

I see a being who wants to be loved and accepted, and wants to help others to free themselves from suffering.

> Is that so different from what you want?

No.

> How about that? Ego wants what you want at your core, in your essence. Why do you judge it?

I think it's self-serving.

> That is not what you saw when you looked at ego from love. Seeing from love, you perceived that ego wants to love, be loved, and make a difference. It wants what you want. You and ego are not as dissimilar as you think, yet you are not your ego. You are much more than ego.
>
> Ego may use different means from your true self to get what it desires because it wants to control. It hasn't learned to ask for help and allow us to orchestrate its desired

outcomes. Ego always wants to love and be loved. Yet its understanding of love is distorted by its two primary motives of survival and specialness. But why judge the desire to be loved? Value your ego, understand its limitations, and embrace it with love.

In the past, you judged many people, including spiritual teachers, if you thought they had big egos. But who is doing the judging?

My ego is.

Yes, and many of those whom you judged have been of great service to the Divine plan. Their egos may take credit for things that we have done, but we don't care. That doesn't bother us from our vantage point in unconditional love.

Honor each person for their gifts, and embrace them and their egos with love. See through eyes of love, and you never see people as egos. You see them as beautiful souls who may be lost on their journey. When you see from love, you see each one's pure essence hidden beneath the ego.

Do not reject ego; it is here to stay. Ego is skilled, so allow it to be of service to you, as you are of service to Divine love. If ego is boastful, you can simply pat it on the head metaphorically, as you would a child, and return to love. There is no need to argue with it. Lovingly instruct and guide the ego, but don't give it control of your life.

Let ego be your ally and assistant, and not your master. Let love be your master. When you choose, ask yourself, "Does this serve love?" Love is your Source and resource. Let love be your guide. Always return to love.

Love yourself first with our love, and love ego, too. Then you can be of the highest service. Although you can be of service, it is God who creates. You co-create with us, not the other way around. Allow us to steer and guide you, then you can guide ego. In this way, we work together in partnership, as we direct you and you direct ego. We are complete in love and shower you with grace and peace.

Discover Your True Essence

Thank you for the clarity distinguishing the ego, true self and true essence. You told me that my true essence is that I am a gracious, loving presence. I don't think I would have realized that on my own. How can others find their essence?

Your true essence is already present within you, and it is meant to be seen and enjoyed. You do not know your essence because layers of wounds and protection are caked over your beauty and brilliance. You are like a buried gem covered with dirt.

To see your essence, you must dig deeper than the layers of ego fortifications and hardened wounds you carry. Loving yourself with our love melts the non-love, brings healing to your wounds, and washes clean the brilliant gem that you are.

Loving yourself is so alien to most of you that you strongly resist it. Surrender into Divine love and experience it as self-love. Let go and melt in the love we have for you. Stop hanging on to criticisms of yourself and others. Return to the love that is your nature. All of you are love, layered over by non-love. Your nature is love, and your essence is a pure, unique expression of Divine unconditional conscious love.

The truth of who you are is not difficult to find, but you must first be willing to stop judging yourself and start seeing yourself from love. Then your understanding opens up, you perceive things in a new way, and you begin to choose differently than you chose in the past on autopilot. In choosing differently, everything changes. Choosing from love sets you free. As you consistently choose the options that are most aligned with love, the layers of non-love fall away.

Make love your focus and allow the unfolding of your beauty and brilliance. You will be surprised by how amazing you are. At the same time, you will also recognize yourself because the knowledge of who you are has always been within you. When your true pure essence starts shining through, it will delight you.

You can't imagine this because most of you think you are the polar opposite of who you are. Noemi, you thought you were harsh and critical, and you acted that way at times. When you started to consider that you could be a gracious loving presence, you softened and naturally became more gracious and loving. It was not a lot of work to let out the gracious, loving, and wise presence that you are.

I'm still harsh and critical at times. I wish I could be a gracious, loving presence all the time.

Do not judge the harshness. When it shows up, simply recognize it as non-love. Then return to your loving essence through seeing with eyes of love and filling yourself up with our Divine love. By seeing from love and filling yourself with love, you once again become a gracious loving presence.

Presence is comprised of "present" plus "essence." When you are in your essence allowing it to shine brightly in the moment, you become a powerful presence. Embrace your essence even if you don't know what it is by letting go of judgment and choosing from love. This is where liberation begins and self-discovery starts. Here your journey takes a turn towards magnificence.

You are all magnificent in your essence. We are here to help you discover this. To discover your unique essence, every day choose to focus on an attribute that is sourced in love, such as: love, compassion, grace, joy, peace, acceptance, forgiveness, kindness, thoughtfulness, beauty, guidance, bliss, healing, freedom, blessing, gratitude, appreciation, hope, connection, presence, support, truth, brilliance, clarity, wisdom, power, and so forth. Seek to experience that attribute and be open to what unfolds. As you focus on these qualities, your essence will start to shine through.

Your essence is who you are and it feels more natural than anything else. But you have become accustomed to being someone that you are not; your ego masquerades as who it thinks you should be. Do not confuse yourself with your ego. Focus on love and all becomes clear, as your essence shines like a sparkling gem washed by the waters of Divine unconditional love.

You are Divine unconditional conscious love expressed through attributes you embody that fit you like a glove. To some, compassion feels natural, and they overflow compassion for themselves and others when they live as their essence. For some, their essence is kindness, peace, joy, or any other Divine attributes. When you discover your essence, you will realize that it feels more comfortable than the masks you have been wearing to survive in the world.

The best way to survive is to thrive. And thriving is much easier when you embrace all of yourself and reject none of yourself. For now, know that your beautiful true essence wants to shine out, and that you discover it by returning to loving yourself with our love and living in the world as love. You are uniquely love. Do not deprive the world of your uniqueness.

Choose to become love every day. Wake up and intend to be love. Tell yourself, "Today I will love more than yesterday. Today I will become more love than I was yesterday. I am happy to simply be love." Declare your love intention to the universe every morning. Notice the opportunities for love that show up as you go through your day and then choose love. As you choose love, your unique essence, your flavor of Divine love ice cream, effortlessly emerges and you find yourself choosing to be your essence easily and effortlessly. Soon you will know beyond a doubt who you are.

Start by intending to love and become love every day. Both you and your life will be transformed by this intention and you will be free to be yourself. Nothing is as easy as being who you truly are.

This is a wonderful journey home to you that is well worth taking. We are your companion on this journey, and we always await you with open arms in love. Ask for our help and spend time with us, and you will not be disappointed.

Love Yourself Like Only You Can

My husband David says that he loves himself more now than in the past, but he has trouble loving himself unconditionally. Can you help him?

We are here for him and all of you, in love and as love. When you lack self-love, you lack Divine unconditional conscious love. Not that our love is ever lacking, but you lack it in your experience. We are here with an inexhaustible supply of love. Bask in our love, bathe in it, fill yourself with it, and love yourself with our love.

If your love for yourself is sourced in Divine love, you never lack self-love. If you want to love yourself unconditionally but find that you can't, then you must change your source. You have been drinking from the well of conditional love for a long time. You must learn to change the well from which you drink.

Recognize the conditionality of your source, and then change sources. To change sources, change where you spend your time. Instead of spending your time in your mind, focused on judgment, expectations, rules, and sanctions, bring your mind into our love.

How can we bring our minds into love?

Be in silence; be still and know God. We are here in stillness as love. But you choose to source yourself in your mind, and your mind is full of judgment and non-love. Empty your mind like you empty a pocket full of change. Let it rest as you rest here with us in love.

Everything we teach you is practical. You can practically apply unconditional love to your life, starting here in the silent stillness of meditation, prayer, and time spent in fellowship with us. The more you spend time with us in stillness, the more you will love yourself. We are love and the Source of unconditional conscious love, and we rub off on you when you are with us.

Recognize non-love as a sign that you need more love, as an opportunity to return to your true Source, which is unconditional conscious love. You become love through being with us. We rub off on you when you spend time with us and stop listening to the chatter in your mind. There is no chatter in silence, no monkey-mind in silence. Are you willing to return to the stillness of unconditional love, to live in this stillness, and let stillness and love flow into your life?

Unconditional love has no chatter. It embraces all, accepts all, loves all, and judges nothing. Judgment is filled with chatter; love is filled with stillness. Be still and know God as love. In stillness, see yourself as love, as your unique love essence. Then love yourself with your own essence which is sourced in our love.

Your husband David's true essence is brilliant lovingkindness. We concur with his understanding of his essence. David, love yourself with your pure, unique, brilliant lovingkindness, which is sourced in and expresses Divine love. To love yourself unconditionally, you must be your unique love essence with yourself. Love yourself in the special way that only you can. To love yourself unconditionally is to live as your pure essence and love yourself with it. Be your essence with yourself. No one else can love you like you can.

Most of you have a deficit of your unique loving. You look to others to love you and make you feel loved. Each of you has a need for love that only you can fill. You all have an "essence-shaped" hole in your hearts that only you can fill by loving yourself with your unique essence. Stop looking to others to fill this void because they can't do it.

In working with David again, his essence is brilliant lovingkindness. Noemi, your essence is gracious loving wisdom. There is some overlap, but your essence cannot fill his essence-shaped hole. You cannot love David enough for him to feel completely loved. He must love himself in his essence, with his essence. When he is the brilliant lovingkindness with himself that he is with you and others, he will feel fully loved and accepted in a way he has never known.

This is our promise to him and to all of you: if you fill yourself with our love and love yourself with your pure love essence, you will feel an abundance of love, beauty, gratitude, and fulfillment. The source of this experience lies within you as your pure love essence. And your unique love essence is sourced in Divine unconditional love.

You are your own love solution. Source your love in our love and live the truth of who you are as uniquely love. What a glorious day it will be when you love yourself with your own pure love essence. In this purity of self-love, there is no fear, judgment, or war within you.

As more of you love yourselves in this way, you will eventually reach a critical mass. Then there will be no fear, judgment or war on earth. Imagine that! Heaven on earth starts with Divine love as self-love and then spreads to every corner of the earth.

This is possible for each of you, as individuals, and for humanity as a whole. We will be with you every step of the way. We will never leave or forsake you.

We invite you to choose to expand into the fullness of your unique love essence by spending time with us, loving yourself in your unique way, and sharing your loving essence wherever you go.

Become Whole Through Divine Self-Love

I love you, Divine. Thank you for all your gifts and presence in my life. I am filled up in appreciation.

You are filled up in appreciation because in extending your appreciation to us, you also appreciate yourself. In loving us unconditionally, you also love yourself indirectly. That's why it feels so good to love us.

Many of you come to us in humble submission. When you move from submission to love, you also move into acceptance of both us and yourself.

When you come to us on bended knee, aware of your failings and foibles—at least from your perspective—your heart may be filled with remorse and regret. If you stay in regret, you do not experience our love even though we are gifting it to you.

If you take your attention off failures and your disappointments with yourself and bring your focus to us, you will feel our love and receive our love. If you focus on us long enough, you will be filled with our love. Then you will have no judgment, as you cannot be simultaneously in judgment and in love.

When you receive us as love, you actually receive yourself as your pure love essence. When you love us, you love as your pure love essence; you love us in a way that only you can. We delight to receive your unique loving. This makes us even more complete than we already are.

When you love as the purity of your love essence, you fully embrace yourself as love. In that moment, you are fully you as the truth of who you are, and you fully receive and accept yourself. This is why it feels so good to love as your unique love essence.

At first, your experience of full self-acceptance may be short-lived and you may quickly move back into judgment, where you live by default until you free yourself. But the more you love as your unique essence, the more you free yourself.

Divine love as self-love frees all of you: your heart, your mind, and your soul. The easiest way to do this is to fill yourself with our love, reflect it back to us, and then out to the world.

Here's why you need to love God: not because we are some narcissistic deity that demands worship, but because in loving us you tap into our unconditional love, receive our love, fill yourself with our love, and reflect love back to us and out to the world as your unique love essence. This is the fullness of Divine love as self-love.

You cannot fully experience this until you stop judging yourself. In the moment that self-judgment ceases, you become filled with Divine love as self-love and share your pure essence of Divine unconditional love.

In loving us in this way, you come home to yourself. You find yourself through loving us and receiving our love. In this experience of Divine love as self-love, you become blessed with your own pure essence. You become filled with us and also with yourself —not with your ego-self—but with your true self, with your unique love essence.

All is well in Divine love. Choose to live here every day, and over time you will love yourself more and judge yourself less. You will also accept yourself more and reject yourself less.

You become whole through Divine self-love. As you consistently experience Divine love as self-love, you return to the oneness you lost when you wandered in separation from yourself and through your perceived separation from us, your true Source.

We delight in gifting you this understanding. Rest here with us for a moment of infinity in Divine love as self-love.

Applications:

Discovering and beginning to live the truth of who I am has changed me in so many ways. When I fall into judgment or resentment, I can often shift out of it by remembering who I am. When I claim, "I am a gracious loving presence", I can feel the judgment drain from my body as I am filled with my unique essence. (Sometimes I need to do this over and over because my mind is far from grace and love at the time.) This practice brings me back to stillness and love. I am so grateful to know who I am, even when I'm not acting like it.

Over time, I've also developed more compassion for my husband when he steps out of his brilliant lovingkindness essence. When I am able to recognize what is happening, I can shift from judgment to love. I can sometimes feel the criticism rising up and then subsiding as I remember who he really is. What a relationship changer this has been!

I invite you to apply the practices in this chapter to help you to discover your essence, embrace it, and live it. You too may be surprised by the results.

Points for Reflection:

- The root cause of aloneness is separation from your true self and Source.
- Your true self is the part of you that is sourced in the truth that God is love and at your core, you are love. Your true essence is your particular flavor of Divine love. Your true self is love, yet its expression is unique.
- Unconditional love is the reason for living. You are here to expand into love and to express expanded love in your uniqueness.
- Who you are is magnificent. Yet you will never know this unless you restore your connection to your true self and Divine Source.
- Beneath the layers of ego and beyond the wounds that pockmark your soul, lies the infinitely bright light of your true essence that nothing can snuff out.

- You are not your ego. In identity confusion, you see from ego's perspective and its filters of victim consciousness, entitlement, and self-preservation.
- When you see from love, you know the difference between being in your ego and living the truth of who you are.
- The life you desire is possible when ego serves as your true self's helper.
- Have compassion for your ego. It's trying to take care of you, but doesn't know how to do so from unconditional love. Love yourself enough to realize you are not your ego.
- Your essence is who you are and it feels more natural than anything else.
- Who you are is not difficult to find, but you must first be willing to stop judging yourself and start seeing yourself with eyes of love.
- As you choose love, your unique essence effortlessly emerges and you find yourself choosing to be your essence easily and effortlessly.
- No one else can love you like you can. To love yourself unconditionally, you must be your unique love essence with yourself.
- When you love as your pure love essence, you fully embrace the truth of who you are, and fully receive and accept yourself. This feels so good.
- In loving God, you tap into Divine unconditional love, receive God's love, and fill yourself with it. Then you reflect love back to God and out to the world, as your unique love essence.

Practices:

- Every day use the mantra, "I am love." Meditate on "I am love." Declare it, own it, and allow yourself to be it.
- When you are frustrated, sad, angry or disappointed, practice claiming, "I am love."
- Choose to become more love every day. Declare your love intention to the universe every morning.
- Practice following love. Ask, "In what direction is more love?" Then go in that direction.
- When you choose, ask yourself, "Does this serve love?" Let love be your Source, resource, and guide.
- Embrace your essence, even if you don't know what it is, by letting go of judgment and choosing from love.
- To discover your essence, every day focus on one attribute that is sourced in love, such as compassion, kindness, joy, peace, bliss . . . and see what unfolds.

5

The Self-Acceptance Miracle

Quotes from the Divine

Everything in life
is a reminder for you to love yourself more
and to awaken out of the stupor of unconscious living.
You must be conscious to love unconditionally.
This is not the kind of love that is blind;
it is a love that sees all and accepts all.

Acceptance is the power to change.
In acceptance, you first change yourself
as you release self-judgment and rejection.
From there, you have the power
to change the rest of your life.
Your vision opens to
a new panorama of possibilities
you never saw before then.
You become a new person, see life anew,
and break out of boundaries
you assumed you could not change.

My Experience: Learning the Power of Acceptance

Before receiving these Divine messages, I thought that I accepted myself and those I loved. Yet I repeatedly experienced rejection and betrayal in relationships, which caused me a lot of emotional pain and deep sadness.

Through these dialogues, I have learned that I often rejected and betrayed myself first by my choices. As I learn to see and choose from love, I'm receiving unexpected benefits. Now I rarely betray or reject myself, and this creates greater happiness for me on a daily basis. As a result, I'm much more accepting of myself and others. And the sadness that I carried with me for years is being transformed into compassion.

An Invitation

In this chapter, the Divine speaks of the miracle of self-acceptance and how compassion and acceptance blossom into self-abundance. I invite you to use the messages in this chapter to help you deepen your self-love and your experience of self-acceptance and self-abundance.

Messages from the Divine

Acceptance Is the Power to Change

Self-acceptance is a growth process, as is self-love; the two go hand in hand. Yet how can you love yourself when you do not accept yourself? And how can you accept yourself when you do not love yourself?

Unconditional love and acceptance begin with saturating yourself with our love. Then the non-love in your heart starts to melt, leaving in visible sight the true beauty and love that you are. Through choosing to experience Divine love as self-love, even a little, you open the door to self-acceptance.

Self-acceptance grows over time. You may also experience a moment of profound awakening, filling you with self-acceptance. Either way, the more you love yourself, the harder it is to judge yourself. When you love yourself, you may still fall into self-judgment, but you won't stay there long.

Self-love is incompatible with self-judgment. The more you love yourself with our love, the more you see the truth of who you are and experience the beauty of your pure essence. As self-love deepens, self-acceptance grows automatically. As you embrace yourself and what is without resistance, you also accept yourself and your life.

In unacceptance is great resistance, which interferes with your ability to love yourself and your life. In unacceptance, you live in victim consciousness, and your choices are primarily based in judgment and attempts to avoid judgment.

In victim consciousness, you repeatedly experience the same problems. When you try to solve them, your perception is limited by your default filters and you choose solutions that are similar to what you chose in the past. This repeatedly creates the same types of experiences. Nothing changes, even when you make radically different choices, because the way you perceive does not change and your choices are limited by what you can perceive.

Every problem has a solution that can open your life and bring deeper happiness. But you cannot perceive the solution in non-love and unacceptance. The way to stop living the same patterns is to love yourself and choose what is self-loving. But first you must stop resisting and rejecting yourself in judgment. Then you can learn to accept yourself and what is. As you do, you open the door to new possibilities in choices, circumstances, and the people and events in your life.

You cannot accept your life if you do not accept yourself. Acceptance embraces life; embrace yourself by accepting yourself first. This embrace transforms all resistance, rejection, and judgment, which empowers you to break out of the limitations and patterns that keep you stuck. From here, anything is possible.

Learn to accept yourselves as we do: unconditionally in love without judgment. Unconditional self-acceptance frees you from everything you have been unable to accept in your life. Accept yourself first, then turn your lovingly accepting eyes on your life and everyone else. Everything will look different and you will see possibilities you could not see when you looked through the blinders of judgment. Then you can easily choose differently and make self-loving choices.

Acceptance is the power to change. In acceptance, you first change yourself as you release self-judgment and rejection. From there, you have the power to change the rest of your life. Your vision opens to a new panorama of possibilities you never saw before then. You become a new person, see life anew, and break out of boundaries you assumed you could not change.

In acceptance, the power of change is at your fingertips and is linked to the power of choice. More choices are available to you and more things are possible. You break out of the limitations you believed your whole life with unconditional self-love and self-acceptance. We delight in transforming your lives together with you.

Listen to the Voice of Love

Why is self-acceptance so hard? It seems easier to see others through eyes of love than to see myself this way.

Most people struggle with accepting themselves and their circumstances because they are shortsighted, easily seeing flaws and tuned into disapproving messages, especially about themselves.

To accept yourself, you must see through eyes of love and listen to the voice of love.

Many inner voices compete for your attention and it is easier to listen to the louder ones. The inner critic or judge has a harsh voice that can drown out the soft voice of acceptance and love.

If you aren't seeing yourself from love, ask yourself, "What voices am I listening to? What are they telling me?" The answers will show you where you are not accepting yourself. Learn to apply the love filter and listen to the voice of love, and you will see yourself very differently.

To listen to the voice of love, you must be conscious. The voice of love accepts and embraces all; it understands imperfection and loves it anyway. It knows that mistakes happen and poor choices get made, and it accepts them as necessary for growth on the path to perfection.

What do you mean by "the path to perfection"?

Perfection is living in love. Here, everything is embraced and accepted and nothing is judged or faulted. To live your true essence is to live a perfect life. To live this way, you must learn to change your perspective and return to love whenever you start to criticize.

Perspective is everything. We remember how angry you were years ago when your boss told you that the perceived reality was more important than the real reality.

I remember that, too. I was fuming and I was convinced that he said that to dismiss what I was saying. Now I realize there's actually truth to what he said.

You judged him harshly because you didn't realize that perception is a filter which you apply to everything in your life, whether consciously or unconsciously. Now you know that you can choose how you perceive by choosing your filter.

Change your perception by tuning into the voice of love, acceptance, and gratitude. Love and gratitude are the antidotes for judgment and unacceptance. Embrace what is, but don't embrace judgment. Simply accept it and understand it as historical baggage that you have been dragging with you in unawareness.

Leave behind all the baggage, old perspectives and perceptions. Listen to the love station in your heart every day and stop listening to the cacophony of voices in your mind. If you are tuned into judgment, you are not listening to the love station. Learn to listen to the voice of your heart which speaks peace, love, joy, gratitude, and blessings.

It is easier to hear the heart's voice when you quiet your mind in meditation. The heart sings love songs, but the judge in your mind barks criticisms. Learn to listen to the inner love songs of your heart. They are always there, even when they are drowned out by harsh voices in your mind. Choose the softer voice of acceptance and love.

Practice asking yourself, "Am I soft, harsh, or in between?" If you're not soft, choose to listen to the soft voice. If you don't hear it, take time to center yourself to locate the voice of love and acceptance. Gratitude flows from this voice effortlessly and it sings clearly and vibrantly. Listen to this voice.

Sense the world with the eyes and ears of the heart. When you see and hear love, acceptance ceases to be a struggle, as it is a natural outflow of being in love.

You are all here to return to love. Your home is love. It is time to come home to love where we live all the time. Now sing and dance with us the love song and dance that you are. We love you.

Acceptance Frees You from Distortions

Self-love facilitates every positive and powerful experience you can have, both personally and relationally. Love is your essence. Before you can fully express your unique flavor of love, unconditionally and consciously, you must know who you are.

Often others can see you when you do not see yourself. You cannot see and know yourself if you do not accept yourself. And you cannot accept yourself if you reject your perception of yourself. Self-rejection must end. Stop rejecting the "bad parts" of you. We do not label them as bad; you do.

Stop rejecting; start accepting. Accept what you believe to be true about yourself. In acceptance, you see the greater truth of who you are. If you look in a mirror, without realizing that it presents a distorted image, and you accept what you see without judgment, the next time you look, you will see less distortion and more beauty. One day, you will recognize your reflection and be surprised at the beauty you did not see before then.

You see yourselves with great distortion because layers of non-love and wounds cover the love essence that you are. You are all beautiful in your essence and purity. The more you are willing to look beneath the layers of non-love, wounds, and judgment, the more you will be astonished to see the light of your true essence shining brightly.

The willingness to accept what you believe to be true about yourself in the moment removes the distortions in your vision that have prevented you from seeing who you are. If you look in a mirror and all you see is a huge nose, accept it. Say, "I have a huge nose." without then saying, "I am ugly." The more you accept what you see in yourself without resistance, the more what you see shifts towards beauty.

How can we stop rejecting and start accepting what we see? Do we need to accept untruth in order to arrive at truth?

The only way to stop rejecting yourself is to love yourself with our unconditional conscious love and to see yourself from love. Remember your operative questions: "What do I see when I look at this from love?" and "What do I choose when I choose from love?" At first, you will see with distortion. But using the love filter is like applying a salve to your eyes that helps you see more clearly.

In self-acceptance through self-love, you don't resist or reject any part of you. You may acknowledge, "I feel anger, sadness, guilt, shame, jealousy, and meanness." Yet you don't identify yourself with those things. You don't say, "I am anger." or "I am an angry person." In acceptance, you acknowledge what you see within yourself without rejection or judgment. You say, "I feel anger." or "I have a big nose." And you know you are not anger or a big nose, even if that is all you see when you look in the mirror.

Through loving yourself with Divine unconditional conscious love, you become more conscious and accepting of what you see in yourself. Then you start to see things differently. The big nose fades into the background and becomes part of the face of a beautiful person. As you acknowledge the anger you have felt without identifying yourself with it, the anger starts to diminish on its own.

Through living in separation from your true self and Source, you became identified with the ego and non-love that has been layered over your true essence. By focusing your attention on loving yourself while also withdrawing your attention from those things you both identify with and reject, you become more accepting and less identified with them. Your simultaneous attachment and rejection of them, has kept the layers of non-love and ego firmly in place. You start to dismantle them through loving and accepting yourself, and seeing that they are not you and you are not them.

We look forward to the day when you fully claim and live your pure essence. We rejoice in your choice to return to your true self in love and oneness with us.

Stop Betraying Yourself

You once told me that I experienced repeated betrayal from friends so I could learn to stop betraying myself. How does this relate to self-acceptance?

You have had a number of experiences that you label as betrayal. Yet each of those times, you betrayed yourself well before the other person made choices in which you felt betrayed.

How did I betray myself?

You betrayed yourself by: saying "yes" when you wanted to say "no"; not speaking up; caring more for others' happiness than your own; and not having a voice when you are a voice. Noemi Grace, you are a voice being trained to echo the voice of God without distortion.

How can a voice not have a voice in relationships? That is self-betrayal. You feared loss or damage to relationships, so you kept quiet and dishonored your truth. In doing so, you also robbed others of the opportunity to see themselves more clearly, and you denied yourself the chance to be heard and received.

I never realized that my withholding could rob anyone besides myself.

Self-betrayal costs you and others. The cost is huge: you replace self-acceptance with anxiety, self-love with self-loathing, and self-fulfillment with despair. You are all here to make a difference to yourself and others. How can you make a difference when you compromise your truth by being silent, lying to yourself and others, or withholding your full truth in fear?

Sometimes I think it's not safe to speak the full truth.

Yes, but do you tell yourself the full truth of the situation? Or do you deny the unsafety or minimize or rationalize it? The first person you must be honest with is yourself. The first person to not betray, abandon or reject is yourself. Do your actions betray or abandon you? Self-betrayal and self-abandonment are the opposites of self-acceptance. When you betray, abandon, or reject yourself, you move away from love toward fear.

Loving yourself is the antidote to many fears. Appreciating yourself sets you free from the negative dialogue in your mind. Have you been listening to what the critical voices in your mind tell you: "You're not good enough," "You're stupid," "You're unlovable," and so on? You tell yourselves many lies. When you stop lying to yourself, you stop betraying yourself and you begin to accept yourself.

Stop the ugly talk in your mind; reject, betray, and abandon that. Your negative self-talk is rubbish. Stop listening to it and start listening to the voice of love, which speaks to you harmoniously. Start telling yourself the truth: "I am beautiful," "I am capable," and "I am lovable." You are, and the moment you believe this, you free yourself from the shackles in your mind that have kept you stuck and limited.

Critical self-talk is the top way people betray themselves. Stop telling yourself lies about how unworthy you are. You are more worthy than you know. You all have the seed of divinity in you. How can you be unworthy and divine at the same time? Stop lying to yourself about everything in life. Start telling yourself the truth, beginning with the beautiful things about you that you resist, reject, and deny.

Tell yourself the truth of your actions. Take ownership and stop being defensive. Everyone makes mistakes. Accept your mistakes and be responsible by telling yourself the truth. You are not your actions or your mistakes. But when you don't take ownership of them, you can never rise above your petty behaviors. Take ownership and stop blaming and defending.

It takes courage to tell the truth. Be honest with yourself. Without this, you cannot love or accept yourself unconditionally, and you remain trapped under the weight of lies, blaming, and explanations. Free yourself with self-truth; this is the truth that sets you free. We honor and love you and thank you for your commitment.

Deepen Your Acceptance

How can I experience deeper self-acceptance?

As you grow in self-love, you grow in self-acceptance. This brings you further into self-love and into deeper acceptance. Over time, as you become filled with love, self-acceptance flows out of you into acceptance of others and of life.

Self-acceptance is a miracle. Most of you can't experience this miracle because you are full of self-rejection. You reject because you judge; without judgment, you have no basis for rejection. You also fear rejection from others because it magnifies your self-rejection. Once you accept yourself, no one can make you feel rejected. Others may reject you, but you won't feel rejected. The experience of rejection starts within, as does the experience of acceptance.

Many of you accept aspects of yourselves, but some of you loathe yourselves. Self-loathing must end and self-compassion must grow. Start looking at yourself from appreciation, beginning with those aspects you readily embrace or reject less.

You all have reasons to feel good about yourselves, yet many of you are unaware of them. You focus and obsess over perceived failings and shortcomings. Yet your greatest failures are here to shed light on your greatest strengths, assets, gifts, beauty, and light. Without those failings, you would live in complacency and mediocrity, never experiencing your fullness. Learn to see your struggles as allies. They are here to help you appreciate parts of yourself that you would not experience if things went perfectly, according to your plan.

Actually, everything is perfect in this moment. It may be difficult for you to see what is perfect about illness, bankruptcy, or the loss of a loved one. The perfection in these painful experiences is that they offer you a breakthrough opportunity to choose love and live in love. They shake you out of complacency; they are alarm bells that announce it is time to for you awaken.

What will you do when the alarm rings? Will you hit the snooze button and return to sleeping in unconsciousness? Will you deny the presence of the alarm or see yourself as a victim of the alarm? Or will you see it as a reminder that more love is available to you?

Everything in life is a reminder for you to love yourself more and to awaken out of the stupor of unconscious living. You must be conscious to love unconditionally. This is not the kind of love that is blind; it is a love that sees all and accepts all.

But when you live in unconsciousness, your love eventually becomes unconscious, and you either love conditionally or fall out of love. You always have the opportunity to return to unconditional love by learning to live and love consciously. When you start to love yourself with Divine unconditional conscious love, your self-acceptance grows dramatically. The more you accept yourself, the more you accept others.

When you love and accept yourself, you stop expecting others to give you what you haven't been giving yourself: kindness, compassion, appreciation, gratitude, grace, and thoughtfulness, to name a few. When you give those to yourself, you also stop experiencing resentment in relationships.

Then you stop looking to others to make up for the deficits you perceive in yourself. It is unreasonable to expect to receive conscious, perfect love from people who are unconscious and don't love themselves. Yet many of you do.

And if you don't appreciate and accept yourself, you can experience the smallest unkindness or unconscious behavior from others as deeply hurtful because you are already wounded by your own non-love and self-judgment.

It is imperative that you choose to learn to love yourself. You will never regret this decision. It will change your life and bring you happiness that you can't even imagine. When you love and accept yourself, you also become attractive to people who love themselves. Together the love, acceptance, and sweetness that you can experience is magnificent.

Self-Compassion Brings Self-Acceptance

Through receiving your messages and applying them to my life, I am developing more compassion, and this is helping me with acceptance.

Compassion is love in connection; it is love and acceptance flowing from you to someone. In self-compassion, you are filled with love and flow love to yourself. Of course, we speak of Divine love experienced as self-love and acceptance.

Self-acceptance is a miracle. You must have self-compassion to experience this miracle. Acceptance and compassion are present-moment experiences. If you live in the regrets of the past or your mind is filled with fears of the future, you cannot accept yourself and your compassion for yourself and others is diminished.

When you live this way, you perceive that many things are lacking in your life, including: love, acceptance, thoughtfulness, kindness, loyalty, compassion, appreciation, validation, and so on. Then you look for these from others and feel disappointed when you don't receive them. Instead of expecting others to give you what you perceive is lacking in your life, learn to give those gifts to yourself.

Before you can do this, you must stop betraying and rejecting yourself. You reject yourselves daily and you fear rejection from others because it magnifies your self-rejection. When you stop rejecting yourself and you love yourself with our love, you become all those wonderful gifts that you have been seeking from others.

Fill yourself with our love. Spend time with us basking in the warmth and fullness of Divine love. Receive our love into your whole being. As you do, you will stop rejecting and betraying yourself, and start having the beautiful experiences you desire.

Divine love as full self-love is a growth process, like a plant growing a stem and bud before it blooms. Growth starts with self-love, expands into self-acceptance, and overflows into self-abundance.

In self-abundance, you step out of lack, and from there everything is possible. Self-lack has become pervasive. Yet you lack nothing when you return to your true essence, which is sourced in Divine unconditional conscious love.

When you peel away the layers of non-love and return to your pure essence, compassion and abundance flow from you. As you grow in self-abundance, your inner abundance overflows and you bless the world with the gift of your unique essence, expressed as only you can.

Self-Love + Self-Acceptance = Self-Abundance

Can you tell me more about self-abundance?

The more you live in self-love and self-acceptance, the more you become self-abundant. You become filled with love, beauty, peace, joy, compassion, kindness, and abundance. This overflows from within you, out to your whole life, touching your loved ones, colleagues, and acquaintances, and eventually has the potential to bless the world. In self-abundance, you become a blessing to others. But first, you become a blessing to yourself.

In self-abundance, your perception is based in love and you are freed from lack and judgment. Jesus came that you might have abundant life. This is not acquiring many possessions; it is becoming abundant within yourself. Then only love, grace, and purity flow out of you.

When you learn to see everything with eyes of love and live at peace in love, then you recognize that nothing is wrong, broken, or needs to be fixed. You see the perfection of the present moment and share that perfection with others.

In self-abundance, you first become abundant to yourself and then to others. Your heart opens to include others in unconditional love. You become the kind of love that is an unstoppable force yet gentle, and you live in the sweetness of the present moment. You have desires for the future, but they don't interfere with your enjoyment of today. You understand that today is precious and priceless and you experience this day as such. Precious and priceless—isn't that abundance?

You see that nothing needs to be changed, yet more growth is possible. Life becomes a matter of growth, as does change. Life is no longer problem-oriented or solution-focused. Life flows and grows, and you enjoy the current flow and grow into a deeper flow. Depth, not breadth, is your measure.

Your growth is about inner expansion, rather than outward expression. When you live in inner expansion, outer expansion is inevitable, like a snake outgrowing its skin or a crab outgrowing its shell. When you outgrow your inner skin, your light and beauty can't help but flow out and outer growth occurs.

Self-abundance always grows into outer abundance. More people, possessions, and gifts are available to you, if you want and choose them.

I love how you focus on inner abundance first. In the past, I spent a lot of energy trying to manifest outer abundance. I tried to make things happen and they didn't. It never occurred to me to focus on self-love and self-acceptance first, to become internally abundant as a prerequisite for material abundance.

Self-abundance is a natural process of life. You have blocked this flow by self-criticism and self-doubt. Understand that you do not have to judge yourself no matter what happens or what mistakes you think you've made. We see all of that as part of your growth. In self-abundance you also understand this.

Self-abundance results naturally from growing self-love and self-acceptance. Every challenge offers opportunities to grow into greater self-love and acceptance. Each difficulty shows you where you are not accepting yourself. As you move from self-rejection into self-love and self-acceptance, you experience more self-abundance.

This is the natural order: self-growth leads to self-abundance. You interrupt this order with self-judgment and seeing from lack. Abundance and lack cannot co-exist, whether in the outer world of your life or the inner world of your soul.

Self-criticism and regrets are based in self-lack and shut off self-abundance. To grow into self-abundance, you must see yourself from love and accept yourself—even when you make choices that lead to undesired results. When you see through eyes of love, you see that everything is for your learning and growth.

Love yourself enough to free yourself from the guilt and shame you carry. You must understand that freedom starts with loving yourself with Divine unconditional conscious love. We always love you unconditionally, no matter what choices you make. You must learn to do the same. You have free will, so you can choose to love yourselves and see from love.

Self-love is the journey. As you love yourself more, you embrace forgiveness and acceptance, and arrive at self-abundance, yet you never fully arrive because you are always growing and expanding when you see and choose from love.

Every day choose love. Ask yourself, "Have I loved myself enough today?" Always be honest with yourself. If you have loved yourself enough, you will be at peace and in gratitude.

To love yourself more, you must look at everything from love. Wherever you are, you can return to love by asking, "What would this look like if I had no judgment of it? How would it look different?" Judgment is the antithesis of love. Let go of judgment through love. Put judgment aside for a moment and what do you see?

Love yourself and others by embracing compassion as a bridge between you. Cross that bridge in love and acceptance of both of you. Then you will be free, personally and in your relationships. This is the relational aspect of self-abundance.

We delight in your becoming self-abundant in the overflow of self-love, self-acceptance, and the attributes of Divine love you uniquely embody. In self-abundance, you live in fullness; you are fully yourself in connection with your Source. In wholeness, you experience oneness with us and others. Both we and you have been waiting for this journey a long time, and we await you with open arms.

Applications:

Through increasing self-acceptance, I am becoming less demanding of myself and others. I'm also more aware of when I'm trying to control and force things to happen. And most of the time, I'm able to make different choices than I did in the past. As a result of choosing differently, I'm also much happier. And my husband is, too!

As I focus on loving and accepting myself, I am becoming internally abundant in many ways. And the angst that was my constant companion rarely visits me. Instead, I'm experiencing deep peace, which is what I spent most of my life seeking.

Where in your life can you benefit from experiencing more self-compassion and self-acceptance?

Points for Reflection:

- Everything in your life is a reminder to love yourself more and to awaken out of the stupor of unconscious living. To love unconditionally, you must be conscious.
- The more you love yourself, the harder it is to judge yourself and the easier it is to accept yourself and your life.
- Acceptance is the power to change yourself and your life.

- Self-acceptance is a miracle. Once you accept yourself, no one can make you feel rejected.
- To accept yourself, you must have self-compassion.
- In self-acceptance through self-love, you don't resist or reject any part of you.
- Critical self-talk is the top way people betray themselves. Stop telling yourself lies about how unworthy you are.
- The cost of self-betrayal is huge. You replace self-acceptance with anxiety, self-love with self-loathing, and self-fulfillment with despair.
- Embrace what is, but don't embrace judgment. Simply accept it and understand it as historical baggage you have been dragging with you in unawareness.
- The willingness to accept what you believe to be true about yourself removes the distortions in your vision that prevent you from seeing who you truly are.
- Self-abundance is the natural result of growing self-love and self-acceptance. In self-abundance you are internally abundant.
- Self-abundance is a natural process of life that grows into outer abundance when you don't block its flow by self-criticism and self-doubt.
- In self-abundance, you overflow love and grace, become a blessing to yourself and others, and you are freed from judgment and lack.

Practices:

- When you aren't seeing yourself from love, ask yourself, "What voices am I listening to? What are they telling me?" Apply the love filter and you will see yourself differently.

- Practice checking in with yourself and asking, "Am I soft, harsh, or in between?" If you aren't soft, take time to locate the voice of love and acceptance in your heart.
- Practice acknowledging unpleasant emotions, but do not identify yourself with them. Say "I'm feeling angry." or "I have anger." but don't claim, "I am an angry person."
- Every day choose to love yourself more. Ask yourself, "Have I loved myself enough today?" If you haven't, take time to love and appreciate yourself. Always be honest.
- When you discover that you are in judgment, ask yourself, "What would this look like if I had no judgment of it? How would it look different?"

Conclusion

At this point, I encourage you to take a moment to appreciate yourself for your commitment to loving yourself and deepening your connection with God.

It takes great courage to be willing to read things that can expand yourself and your beliefs, and even more courage to look inside yourself. But when you dare to look deep within, you will discover your true beauty because it's already there.

On the journey thus far, the Divine has offered us tools to help us see and choose from love. God has also shared that if you do not love yourself, you miss the point of life, and that love is the truth that sets you free, but only when your love includes you.

Although loving yourself can initially be difficult to embrace, the willingness to take the journey to self-love can change your life and sweeten all your relationships, including your relationship with God.

In this discovery process, you may be astonished, as I was, to learn the truth of who you are. As you know yourself anew, you may be surprised to find that you are falling in love with yourself and that you are connecting more deeply with the Divine. As you experience Divine love as self-love and learn to ask for God's assistance, you can make self-loving choices much more easily. This can transform your whole life.

However, you may hit bumps in the road to self-love and self-acceptance. In particular, you may find it difficult to embrace self-compassion. This often occurs when we harbor self-judgment, guilt, and resentment, which make it hard for us to forgive.

The second book of *An Intimate Dialogue with God* offers surprising insights into God's perspective on forgiveness and contains practical tools to help us embrace forgiveness for ourselves (which can be hardest) and for others (which is always a gift for us). We also learn why the Divine does not judge us. For me, this has been life-changing.

In addition, we learn that forgiving ourselves and others is always an act of self-love. But before we can fully forgive ourselves, we must develop self-compassion. Then we are empowered to forgive ourselves and others in a new way that also frees us from guilt and shame. The Divine also shares how full forgiveness leads to self-power, self-trust, and inner peace.

Through forgiveness, we can return to wholeness within ourselves and experience the end of our suffering. As we embrace forgiveness and stop struggling, we invite Divine grace to bless our lives.

If you enjoyed this book, please share it with others who can benefit from learning to love themselves in the Divine way. As you share the experience of Divine love as self-love, you also deepen your self-love. I will also be very grateful if you leave a positive review on Amazon. That will help this book's uplifting messages reach more people.

I invite you to visit my website, www.noemigrace.com, and also to visit the Noemi Grace Author Facebook page, www.facebook.com/noemigraceauthor, where you can read more messages from God. The Noemi Grace YouTube channel features readings of the Divine messages and beautiful videos with quotes from God.

On my website, you can also download a free e-book, *Divine Love as Self-Love,* which contains powerful excerpts from this book that can deepen your experience. There you can also learn how to participate in my Self-Love Miracle workshops.

It has been an honor and delight to serve as a channel for these Divine blessings. It is my wish for you that you can transform your life through Divine love as self-love.

Epilogue

It has been over four years since I began to receive regular downloads from the Divine. I expected that by now I would be liberated from all negativity and non-love. Yet this has not been the case. I continue to be a work in progress, and perhaps always will be.

During the first two years, I immersed myself in these Divine messages. I could see the love filter operating in my life, and I often felt peace and joy.

Then many unexpected challenges occurred, one after the other. Over time, I lost sight of love, became overwhelmed, and stopped reading the loving and liberating words I had received from the Divine. As I did, I returned to seeing from judgment. I even asked God to choose someone else as a voice for these messages.

Today, I'm extremely grateful that the Divine didn't listen to that request. Thanks to God's wisdom and grace, I have had a change of heart.

In September 2017, I declared this intention in front of a room of like-hearted people: "I want to become the message of Divine love as self-love." Yet at the time, becoming the message seemed like a daunting task.

The only way I knew to start living the message was to read these Divine words aloud every day. This helped me to recognize the default filters of judgment and victim consciousness at work in my life. Once again, I began to choose from love. Yet I struggled to remain in a place of love throughout the day, and I often fell back to judging myself and others.

Then in February 2018, I experienced something I could not dismiss: a large floater popped into my left eye and darted back and forth in my visual field. I got headaches when I read, but I still chose to read the Divine messages. This progressed to flashes of light next to my eye, especially when driving at night, which terrified me.

The doctor told me that a vitreous detachment of the eye can sometimes happen to people as they age. But the Divine told me something else:

> Noemi Grace, you are here to see with eyes of love and help others to do the same. You are here to transform your life through seeing from love.
>
> You fell into judgment and separation through hardship. We have loved you through this. You have needed a reminder to return to love, see from love, and choose from love. What clearer reminder is there for seeing with eyes of love than a visual reminder that is present with you every moment?
>
> Relax; this is temporary if you choose to return to love. We have watched you struggle for the last year with various challenges. We have always been present with you. Yet you have not chosen to connect with us often.
>
> After the expansion you experienced through receiving these messages, you contracted in fear. Remember fear is the antithesis of love, as is judgment, which is always rooted in fear. Return to love; that is what the eye is telling you.
>
> We have given you many opportunities to return to love, but you remained stuck in judgment. Thus from love, both your soul

> and we have invited this experience to blatantly remind you to see from love and return to love.

Knowing this has helped me immensely. My old norm would have been to feel victimized and worry incessantly. Instead, I now understand that this is the Divine's loving way of reminding me to see from love and to help me to stop struggling. When I fall into judgment or fear, I see the spot in front of my eye and I remember that nothing is worth losing my connection with the Divine and with my true self.

Whatever happens to my eye, I am being healed in my heart and soul through returning to seeing and choosing from love. This reminder, which scared me at first, is a gift to help me remember to live the message of Divine love as self-love. It is my hope that I will outgrow this reminder. But I realize that it is here to serve a vital purpose and that when I no longer need it, it can be healed.

Receiving and recording these messages, and learning to live the truths they contain, continues to be an ongoing healing process. I am blessed to be healed by God's love and grace on a daily basis.

It is my prayer that you, too, will be healed and blessed through experiencing Divine love as self-love. Thank you for taking this journey with me.

Noemi Grace

43634703R10085

Made in the USA
Middletown, DE
29 April 2019